Angels

PROTECTED ME

Hemiah

All scriptures written in this book are from the King James Version Bible.

Contents

PREFACE

HELLO AMERICA! Get prepared to meet a very remarkable, amazing woman. She is raw but subtle, and she is bodacious but discreet. "The Sexy Teenager," as I so fondly like to describe her, is sharing with you her most precious commodity: her life. I know that you will enjoy reading her book as I enjoyed being her editor.

Milton McDaniel
April 6, 2016

Author's Note

You'll notice in this story I go by three fictitious names: Kamiah, Nancy (my relatives call me by this name, and Vienna (this was my stage name as a nightclub dancer.) Most of the people mentioned in this story have fictitious names to protect the innocent. My four adult children go by their real names: Michael, Patricia, Richard, and Jason.

About The Author

I am a native of California, my family lived in a shotgun house, where I was born. A shotgun house has a hallway from the front door to the back door. It has rooms on both sides of the hallway. My family lived at 20th and Pico in Santa Monica. I had six siblings at that time and I'm the seventh child. I was 1 and ½ years old when the Pearl Harbor blackout of World War II happened in 1941. I remembered my mother telling the family to turn off the lights and to lie down on the floor. We heard the roar of airplanes flying over our house. I could hear guns shooting in the air too. It sounded like the sound of the 4th of July fireworks but louder, I was nursing my bottle walking around in the dark. With one hand in front of me, I was feeling my way around in the dark. All the family was in the living room on the floor. I was trying to find my mother. I felt a hand that pulled me to sit me on the floor. I knew I had to keep quiet. I didn't talk very well at that age. But I knew it was a serious thing happening.

Inspired To Become A Musician

We lived in Henderson, Nevada, in an 8-unit apartment building. It was a lot of desert land near us. That's where my 8 siblings and I would play. We'd slide down the dirt hills on cardboard boxes. In the wintertime, we had snow to play in. We'd slide down the snow on the hills on old tires. Sometimes, we'd throw snowballs at each other. It was so much fun.

It was the summertime of 1945, my parents took me with them to a tent church meeting. I was 5 years old. It was a huge crowd there. The only place we had to sit was on the back row. There was sawdust on the ground for us to walk on. When we first got there, I saw birds flying and chirping at the top of the tent. But when I heard the music coming from the piano, I forgot all about the birds flying around. From that moment on, the music was all I focused on. I couldn't see the person playing the piano because the people in front of me blocked my view. So I stood on the seat of my chair so that I could see who was playing the piano. The sound of the music was so beautiful! That day, I said, I want to be a musician, after I listened to the beautiful music. Nothing else mattered to me then.

At that moment, I saw myself playing the piano one day just like her. I said out loud, I want to be a musician when I grow up. My mother dressed me in my favorite lavender dress. It had 3 tiers of ruffles at the bottom, with puffy short sleeves, and a bow tie in the back. I wore my white patent leather shoes with white socks. She styled my thick long hair with two French braids which hung down to the middle of my back. She put a lavender barrette in my bangs to hold it in place.

When we left that tent meeting service, I was a changed little girl. I couldn't think about nothing else but playing a piano. As soon as we got home, I made a pretend piano; I used clothespins to make the keys for it. I placed them in the window seal. I'd play my pretend piano by pressing the clothespins with my fingers, then I made the sound of music with my mouth. I'd sing, "Ding, ding, ding! When I pressed down on the clothes pins they would pop up and then fall on the floor.

I was 10 years old when my parents bought a piano for the family. When I got to play on the real piano keys, I was so excited. My mother was my first piano teacher. But the most valuable things my siblings and I learned from our parents was the word of God first, then piano lessons.

Encouraged To
Write This Memoir

When I shared with my oldest son that I was writing a book about my life, he was excited about the idea. "Mother, are you going to tell your story like it really was?" "Michael, do you want me to?" "Yes, because it's your history mommy. Don't be ashamed of what happened because your life was planned the way it was supposed to be."

While I was attending the community college, I wrote an essay in my English class. It was about "My Near-Death Experience." After my tutors read it they said my story inspired them. They said it strengthened their faith to know that there's nothing impossible for God to do. They told me that I needed to write a book. After family, friends, and colleagues urged me to write a book, I decided to go ahead and write this book.

Out of all my friends, Margie was the one I've known the longest. When she said to me, "Girl, you need to write your story. She was the first one I let read a small portion of my story. After everyone else told me to write my story, she was the one who put the icing on the cake.

"My Mother's Unique Qualities"
Written by my daughter Patricia Harbin

What makes my mother so unique is her love for God, family, and people.

Nowadays people only think of themselves. My mother has always had a nurturing spirit about her. She loves to see people succeed in life.

She's patient, kind, and understanding, which is what you need to teach children. She is a music teacher, who has seen some of her students go on into the entertainment business. One of her students has her own TV show.

Her smile and laughter are infectious, she brightens up any room. I would go with her to sing and worship the Lord with those who were in the convalescent homes.

She brought smiles to their faces and mine.

So I hope you'll consider my mother for a scholarship, she deserves it.

Sincerely,

Her Daughter,
Patricia Harbin

My daughter wrote this letter for me, so, I could get a chance to win a scholarship to continue my education in music. I didn't win that time, but I haven't given up on pursuing my musical career.

Poem Dedicated To My Children:

Michael, Patricia, Richard, and Jason.

POEM

"ANGELS PROTECTED ME"

I'm in no way proud of my past!

Being a young mother at age 15, was way too fast!

Being so young I didn't know how to be a wife!

At age fourteen, I didn't know how to live an adult life.

When I ran away from home, I wanted to be on my own!

For me life got too rough! I couldn't make it all alone!

I wanted to go back home,

But my parents didn't welcome me!

My mother gave tough love to me,

all because from her rules I wanted to be free!

You made your own bed hard is what she said to me.

Go live your life, be the best woman that you can be!

Now I am guided by God's directions,

that's when angels protect me, that makes the difference!

When I embraced my past, it gave purpose to my history!

I hope it encourages others to write their story!

To GOD, I give him all the glory!

Love Forever, Your Mother,
Minister H. E. M.

I'm Not Perfect
Dedicated to my Children
Michael, Patricia, Richard, and Jason

I'm in no way proud of my past life. Since I promised my children I'd tell my story the way it happened; my oldest son, Michael said, "Mom, don't feel bad about what happened because that's your history." I explained, "Michael I was just a teenager." "Mom whatever happened in your life was supposed to happen so tell it the way it was."

"Well, OKAY, BUT I WASN'T PERFECT." "Mom I love you just because you're my Mommy." All four of my children tell me they are happy that I am writing this memoir. I'm grateful that they have a relationship with me now. Praise Elohim (the Lord.) He is my life.

Our parents Mr. and Mrs. Beckman are deceased. The legacy they leave to the family is the "Word of God." That was the greatest gift we received from them.

"Angels Protected Me," is the title of my story because every time I called on God, He sent angels to protect me. I base this story on Psalm 91:11; it says, "For he shall give his angels charge over me, to keep thee in all my ways."

Praise God! Hallelujah! This is a miracle!

INTRODUCTION

Everybody has a story to tell. Think about it. Write your biography, it may help others with problems they are going through.

When we put God first in our life he directs our path. His angels protect and guide us through our life's journey. According to Psalm 91:11, "For he shall give his angels charge over me to keep me in all my ways. That scripture inspired me to title this story, "Angels Protected Me."

ANGELS PROTECTED ME AT AGE 5

Our family lived in Henderson, Nevada, in 1945 when I was 5 years old. I was on my way to a pre-school that was a half a block away from home. My mother let me walk to school because there were no streets for me to cross. I wasn't afraid to walk to school because I saw my guardian angel flying by my side. This is not a dream, it's a true story. Angels are real spiritual beings.

I'd talk with my guardian angel. After I got to the classroom I'd say goodbye to my angel. Then my angel would disappear. After class was over my angel would return to walk me back home. I'm sharing this story because as far as I know angels have watched over me all my life. It happened to me 72 years ago.

As I share this story, please keep in mind it is to give God all the glory for what he has brought me through. I pray it will bless others to know that God never leaves us nor forsakes us. Even though it took me a long time to realize he was always with me.

I'm sharing with you what God brought me through. As you read it you may find yourself with mixed emotions like I did when I wrote it. I mentally relived my story. It was so painful I had to stop typing so I could cry. My eyes are full of tears. The nightclub story was so frightening, it changed my life forever. I'll never go back to another night club. I also have humorous stories that may make you laugh too.

As you read this story you'll understand how God can turn bad things into good for us. Even though bad things happened to me, I learned valuable lessons from them. I wasn't happy when I went through them. Today, I can say I found joy after sorrow. I can see that if it had not been for the LORD on my side where would I be? I wouldn't be here writing this memoir today.

ACKNOWLEDGMENTS

I give honor to God, who is the head of my life. He is my life. Of whom I give all the glory and the praise for giving me life

LORD, thank you for salvation. LORD, thank you for healing me. Father God, thank you for supplying all my need according to your riches in glory by Christ Jesus. Thank you for giving me the courage to share the good news with others that you love us so much, that you gave your only begotten Son. That whosoever believes in him shall not perish, but shall have everlasting life. I thank you for all these blessings, in Jesus name, Amen.

I thank, Reverend's Walter and Margie Rumford for visiting me while I was ill. Thank you for the errands you ran for me. Thank you for the anointed prayers you prayed over me also. Sister Mary Williams thank you, for providing me with transportation to and from my doctor visits.

Thank you, Sister Sellie, for spending the night in the hospital with me. Thank you, Sister Brim for giving me words of encouragement that brightened my day. Thank you, my sister Darlene for praying for me, and giving me the little book with healing scriptures. My 9-year-old great nephew Austin, anointed my head with olive oil, my health instantly became better. He is my sister's grandson.

Thanks to my great grand-daughter, Qiana, at age 5, who prayed that I would be able to eat food again. I thank God, he answered her sincere prayer. Now I can eat food again.

I thank my family members, relatives, and a host of friends who prayed for me. Thank you to those who sent cards, beautiful flowers, and stopped by to visit and anointed me with oil. Those who brought me laughter. It was like medicine to my soul. I needed a lot of help throughout the testing time on my bed of affliction in 2002.

It's not easy to know where to start, saying the words to express my gratitude. But it comes from the depths of heart. THANK YOU.

Proverbs 18:24, "A man that hath friends must show himself friendly: and there is a friend that sticks closer than a brother."

GOD loves you, and I love
you too.
Minister H. E. M.

GOD OPENS DOORS

When I enrolled in school for music, I just want to learn how to play the piano for fun. I had no idea of where it would lead me to. A lady came to visit my church and she heard me playing the piano. She said that she liked the way I played the piano. Then she asked me would I like to be the musician at her church.

Since I only played the piano once a month at my church, I accepted her offer.

So I started playing the piano for her church—3 Sundays a month. Her husband was the Pastor. One thing led to another. I started teaching one student at a time in my home. My first student was my son Richard. After I started teaching other children my husband didn't like it that I was teaching at home. "You need to teach at a school, "he said resentfully.

He had no idea that that was the key that inspired me to step out on faith to teach at school. I had never taught at a school before. But I was willing to do it. I just needed the opportunity to teach at a school. I knew I'd love it. Before I knew I'd teach in a school I could see myself in a classroom.

It wasn't long after that God opened doors for me. The first year I started teaching at the schools I taught at two private schools to start with then I began teaching at the local community college. Altogether I had three schools to teach at. My students increased from one student at a time to more than five hundred over the years. God blessed me with the gift to teach piano lessons.

I've been self-employed for over 25 years. I thank God for opening the school doors for me. I give Him all glory for it. I'm truly blessed. I was at the right place at the right time. When I stepped out on faith I asked God for wisdom and knowledge to teach each student. He gave it to me.

My husband didn't think I could teach at a school without credentials. When God opened the doors of teaching for me that was all the credentials I needed. God gave me the gift to teach. I just had to equip myself with the musical education first. That I did do.

It inspired me to study the Bible to gain more knowledge of Him. There's nothing impossible for Him to do. We can depend on Him for everything. All we need to do is have faith in Him, and believe that there's nothing impossible with Him.

My husband gave me a difficult time about teaching my students at home. But he had no idea he was doing me a favor.

He didn't like it when the parents dropped off their children in our home for piano lessons. He thought I would be discouraged, if I had no place to teach my students. But it turned out that God gave me something greater. When my husband closed the door for me to teach at home it was the best thing that ever happened to me.

I took it as an opportunity to step out in faith and let God direct my path. But teaching is something I enjoy doing. When school doors opened for me teach piano lessons it shocked my husband.

(According to Romans 8:28, "And we know that all things work together for good to them that love God, to them who are the called according to his purpose.") God gave me the gift of teaching. So that is my purpose her on earth.

I relied on the Holy spirit to guide me as I taught piano lessons. Wow, How awesome! God worked it out for my good when my husband expected it to have a negative outcome for me. But his plan backfired on him. I've learned to just keep the faith in God, while going through my trials and tests.

A PHENOMENAL VISION AT AGE FIVE

Our family lived in Henderson, Nevada, in 1945, there are nine girls and five boys. I'm the fifth girl, and I'm the seventh child in the family. When I was five years old, I had the most phenomenal vision.

My siblings and I were outside playing a game called, "The Little Chocolate Chickens and the Big Bad Wolf!" We used old tires for our play houses. That's where the chocolate chickens hid from the big bad wolf, The tires were laying four feet apart. Whenever we played outside of our tire play houses, the big bad wolf would try to catch us, The person that the wolf caught would become the bad wolf. Then the little chocolate chickens would go back to play. But the wolf had to go away to hide. That was a funny little game. My older siblings created that game.

While playing the game, I heard a soft voice speaking to me. It told me to go into the house. As a result, I obeyed the voice. After going into the house, I went straight to my bedroom. I was on the bed lying on my back. I stretched out my arms into a horizontal position while looking up at the ceiling. I could see into the spiritual world. I have a gift to see things in the spiritual world. It doesn't happen when I want it to; it only happens when God wants to get my attention. The opening in the ceiling was the same size of the bedroom. It was an epic scene.

I saw thousands of angels surrounding Jesus while he was descending from heaven. The light that surrounded them was so brilliant that it lit up my bedroom. Jesus spoke to me, "You and your family will be saved." (He predicted my future when I was only five years old.) When I heard that message, it was the most amazing voice I'd ever heard. Just before the ceiling closed I watched as Jesus and His Angels disappeared into the clouds.

When I returned to the game with my siblings, I couldn't tell them about the vision. I knew they wouldn't understand it. Have you ever had a knowing that there are some things we just don't talk about? My encounter with the LORD was not a dream. It's a true story.

My mother lived in a small county town Porterville, California. I went to visit her on my 68th birthday. She said, she had something to tell us. That was my sister Rhonda, my daughter, and me. She told us about the same vision I had in 1945. She said she saw Jesus and his angels appearing in the sky. She didn't know our visions were the same when it happened to me at age 5. My mother was 98, I was 68 and it was our first time knowing that we had the same vision.

I looked at my sister and my daughter; we were in shock! When our mother told us about her vision. I knew without a doubt she was giving me confirmation to the same vision I had. That was so awesome. At age five, I had no idea what a vision meant. It was like looking at a movie on an epic screen. When it happened, I was wide awake. It wasn't a dream. It was the most amazing thing I ever saw.

We had no idea it was going to be our last visit with our mother. She confirmed that our visions happened on the same exact day.

On November 30, 2008, our mother passed away. I'm so glad I let her know how much I loved her. What I can see from my mother's life and passing away was she completed her journey on earth. Our mother was 98 years old, but she didn't look her age. She taught us if you think old, you will look old. It is so true! There are so many people I've met that do not believe I'm 77 years young.

SPECIAL COMMENTS
FROM FAMILY AND FRIENDS

This is concerning my friend and sister in Christ, Kamiah, whom I have known for 40 years. She has always been a kind, loving, and sweet person. Even though she has been through many challenges in her life, she has not changed as a person. If it was any change it was for the better. She's had many things happen in her life to warrant a change, but she could maintain because of her deep faith in God through Jesus Christ. Now she is even stronger in her faith because of the victories. She's had many physical challenges that I have seen her go through, and I know that only her faith in God could have brought her through. That same faith brought her through many personal dilemmas in her life. I must admit that I probably couldn't have gone through some of the things she endured and still have a stable mind. She is quite an overcomer.

I'm sure some of the challenges she has been through will help others know that there is a blessing on the other side.

Kamiah became a member of our church, place of worship, on October 1, 2001. After three years she expressed to my husband, Pastor Walter Rumford, that she had been called to the Ministry. She became a licensed minister on January 11, 2004, and after many sermons she became an ordained minister on December 16, 2007.

We learned many things from her testimonies about her life. God had been with her since her childhood (where she experienced many dreadful things, a young teenager shouldn't ever have to go through) and had brought her through many trials and tribulations. She would often tell the congregation how she would say to God, Lord you said in your word according to Romans 8:28, "And we know that all things work together for good to them that love God, to them who are the called according to his purpose."

Then she said she would ask God to show her the good that is supposed to come from her painful divorce, and said that God gave her an awesome answer. She said she heard God clearly say to her, "Now you get to know Me." Now, by the grace of God, she is telling her story so others will know how they too can make it and get to know God through His Son, Jesus Christ.

Love you,
Your sister in Christ,
Friends always,
Margie Rumford

LETTERS FROM MY CHILDREN

Dear Mother,

When a child is young, they really don't know or understand what's going on with life or anything else. Children don't get it, until they get older, that what mom was saying all along. Then and only then they respect and love mom more because we may not always agree with each other, but what are you gonna do? At the end of the day they are still your family. God bless our family with lots of love. Love you no matter what. Thank you for your guidance, love of God, and family.

> Your Daughter,
> Patricia.

To My Mother:

Your bloodline is running strong with promising education for all the family.

> From: Your oldest son
> Michael

To Grandma,

I am very proud of you. You have touched many lives throughout the century and gave a helping hand to others. You gave a kind word to help someone through the day.

When I or any of my cousins were wrong, you provided gentle guidance or a switch if needed to keep us in our place. All the wisdom you gained in your years, you passed along with love. I thank you for that.

Most of all, you taught your children about the love of God. I know you taught all of them well because I hear my mother Kamiah, my aunts, and uncles praise the lord. I hear my cousins speak about the lord because of what you shared. I will teach my daughter Krystine about the LORD too. That is a part of the legacy you leave in all our hearts.

> Thank you, Grandma, I love
> you very much.
> Richard L. M.

Chapter 1

ALLENSWORTH, CALIFORNIA

It was in 1947, when my parents moved us to a little town called Allensworth. This town was Black-owned by Colonel Allen Allensworth. The houses were spread out with plenty of space between neighbors. There were two Black-owned grocery stores; the people there grew some vegetables of their own in gardens. Then, I was 7 years old, and in the second grade. I went to the only school that was in our small town. We had one teacher that taught the first grade through the eighth grade. She was also the principal too. All my older siblings and I were in the same classroom.

Our teacher lived in Los Angeles, California. So she had to travel by train from Los Angeles to Allensworth. She'd get there on Sunday on evening. She'd teach at the school Monday through Friday. Then, she'd leave after school on Friday evening to return to Los Angeles to be with her family for 2 days. I remember, our teacher had rough looking skin. She told us that she was burned from a terrible house fire.

She was a nice person, but she had strict rules in the classroom. Now that I've experienced teaching children, I understand, that teachers must set rules in order to have order in the classroom. The teacher had a long switch she kept near her at her desk. If she caught the students whispering to one another, she'd whack them with her long switch. She didn't have to leave her desk to hit us. Wow! it sure would hurt.

One day, I was at school early, so, the teacher let me ring the school bell. I was in the first grade. The bell was so huge it used to let me off my feet while I held the rope tight.

I would have so much fun. I'd laugh every time the bell lifted me off my feet.

I remember, when school was out for the summer, my brothers use to chase us girls

There was plenty of vacant land where we could run and play. Our three brothers would find dead snakes and throw them up in the air at us. Our brothers would laugh at us because we didn't want the snakes to get near us.

Our mother was pregnant with the thirteenth child in the family. It was in 1950 when we moved from there to Bakersfield, California.

Chapter 1a - One Big Family

It was 1950, our mother gave birth to our baby sister in January. A few months had passed, our baby sister was three months old, in the springtime. It was the early part of spring, the birds were chirping in the trees. There were pink and white blossoms blooming on the fruit trees. I am the seventh child out of 13 siblings—eight girls and 5 boys. Our family lived in downtown Bakersfield, California. Whenever there was a parade in town, we would sit on our front porch to watch it. We saw the Christmas and New Year's parade every year from our front porch. That was exciting. One of our older sisters took care of us, while our parents worked. In those days, it wasn't easy to clothe and feed 13 children. To have extra income our parents would take us to work with them during the summertime. We worked in the cotton fields, potato fields, and the fruit orchards too. One day, my father took me along to pick cotton. I complained so much about the cotton bolls hurting my fingers. My father said, oh girl go somewhere and sit down. That made me happy! That was my first and last cotton-picking experience. I sat on my cotton bag the rest of the day. I played the rest of the day with little lady bugs they were orange with black dots on them. I pretended that the bugs were little cars. I was 10 years old then.

My family called me by the name Nancy; however, it wasn't my real name. My third oldest sister changed my name verbally. When I was ten years old, my brother Donnie was eight we were running buddies. We lived in the downtown area of Bakersfield. We'd sit on the front porch of our house catching ladybugs. We didn't have toys so, we'd pretend that the little lady bugs were little cars. We'd make them race by poking them with leaves. We were one big happy family, where there was lots of laughter in our home.

We didn't have toys to play with. But one time someone donated us a brand new bicycle. We took turns riding it. We had a lot of fun. Can you image sharing one bicycle with 12 siblings with various heights. The younger children had to hold their hands high over their head to reach the handle bars. We had to stand up to paddle the bike as we wobbled from side to side. We couldn't sit on the seat to paddle. It was tiring to ride the bike that way. I didn't ride too far, but I had fun anyway. It's a good thing it was a girl's bike, because it made it easier to ride.

Our parents couldn't afford to buy bikes for all of us. Even though we didn't have toys to play with we had a lot of laughter.

We were one big happy family. We had a three-bedroom house. But it wasn't big enough for all of us to have our own room. During night time, we had to sleep with two other siblings in one bed, but we managed. We did a lot of playing before going to sleep.

There were times when our mother would call us from her bedroom she'd say, "All right you kids, you'd better be quiet and go to sleep."

Yes, there was a lot of laughter in our home except the days when I was getting a whipping. To me that wasn't funny. Well, I can say, it seemed like I got whipped every day. Wow Wee! Ouch! My mother used to whip hard. I wished I could die. She used to whip me with an extension cord. and made me remove my clothes. Then she would tuck me under a sheet in the bed. She'd hit my head, my butt, and my back. It didn't matter to her what she hit. It used to hurt so badly. I thought I was going to die.

When we got a chance to go places that was the only time it seemed like I wasn't getting a whipping. Sometimes I'd get into trouble when it was another sibling's fault. They'd be the one starting the fight.

On Sundays, our parents would take us to Isabella Lake to play and fish. It wasn't too far from Bakersfield. My father taught us how to catch fish, but we had to be brave enough to put the worm on the fish hook. I would peek out of one eye at the slimy and wiggly worm hoping it would make it easier for me to touch it. That wasn't much help. It still felt yucky.

Finally, I hooked the worm. My dad gave me a high five as he chuckled with a deep belly laugh. My father was a jolly dad, he liked to tease us a lot. So he would tell me that he would give me a nickel, if I'd put worms on the hook without making funny faces. That was hard to do. Finally, I put the worms on the hook and enjoyed catching the fish. My father said me that I had to get over my fear of fishing because one day I may need to catch a fish for my dinner. From that day on I learned to enjoy going fishing.

Chapter 1b - Secret Get-Away

It was spring time in 1952, I was 12. Our family lived in Bakersfield, California. Our parents drove Donnie and me to the grocery store with them. They had a dark green Hudson car. We'd call it the green watermelon, and we'd say that we were the seeds . We'd get a good laugh about it.

On our way, home our father stopped in front of a furniture store. It was two blocks down the street from where we lived. We lived on 19th and Main Street in the downtown area of Bakersfield. We saw a box-shaped thing from a glass window. It was on a table inside. It had cartoon pictures moving inside of the box. At that time, we didn't know the correct name for the box.

Our mother heard us talking about the box we saw in the window. She knew what it was so, she laughed and corrected us. She said that's not a box you saw, the correct name for it is television. My brother and I laughed so hard. We crinkled our nose as we looked at each other, while grinning. We asked our mother, a television, what's that? It was so funny to us. We had never seen a television before that day. It was so amazing. We had only seen inanimate (lifeless) cartoons in the comic books, or in the newspaper. But that day we saw the cartoons moving inside the television. That was so awesome. On our way home, mom said to dad, "We'll buy a television one day."

I whispered to Donnie, when we get home let's come back to see the cartoons. Ok. He was 1 year and nine months younger than me. When we got home our mother was preparing the dinner. The older siblings were busy helping her. I made plans for Donnie and me to run away from home. We made sure to eat dinner before we left home. We sneaked out of the house as soon as our mother started playing the piano. It was time for family worship that was the time we read the Bible, sang and prayed. We had it every day just before the sun would set. Donnie and I were back at the furniture store.

Chapter 1c - Ran Away From Home

We stood outside of the store, watching cartoons through the window. We couldn't hear a sound, but it was still fun to us. After the cartoons ended, I wondered what to do next. It was getting dark; my little brother was crying. If we went back home we'd get a whipping. I didn't want my brother to know that I was afraid too. I gave him a hug and assured him it would be alright. I didn't know we were going to learn a hard lesson about life. It was worse than a whipping from our parents. As children, we had no idea how hard it would be for us after running away. We had no idea of where we were going to sleep, eat, and live. In addition, we didn't have money to live on.

We had only light clothing. He was wearing a short sleeve shirt and a pair of beige khaki pants. I was wearing a short sleeve floral print dress with ruffles on the hem. After dark, it got cold. I wondered how we'd keep warm. As we walked down the alley, I saw a blanket hanging on a clothesline. I told my little brother to grab it. I kept a look out so he could grab it. After he got the blanket we ran as fast as we could down the alley.

The sun was sinking fast. We hurried to find a place to sleep. I had no idea of all the dangers that existed in the world. We didn't realize home was the best place for us. We didn't know how to take care of ourselves. We kept walking through the alley looking for a place to rest. But every place we stopped we heard noises moving in the bushes. Donnie, what if that is a snake? Our eyes got big with fear as we looked at each other. We held hands real tight, and kept walking fast. He cried. I'm scared." I wanna go back home." I reminded him, if we go home, we'll get a whipping.

Finally, we came to the end of the alley. My heart was beating fast with fear. It was an old rundown auto repair shop at the corner. It looked scary and spooky. There was broken glass lying on the ground because someone had broken the windows. We could see where the paint had peeled off the building. We were getting sleepy, so, we sat next to the old shabby building. Our backs were up against the outside wall. We huddled together under the blanket to keep warm.

I didn't realize we both had drifted off to sleep. The next thing we saw was a flashlight shining in our face, it startled us. "Alright you two, come with me," he said. It frightened us so much we started to cry. The police officer asked, "What are you two doing out here so late?" We don't want a whipping.

The police officer drove us home. I was so afraid my heart was beating fast. I didn't want to get a whipping. I remembered, when I was nine years old my mother whipped me so hard that I wanted to die. She made me to remove all my clothes and lie on the bed with only a sheet covering me. She had the sheets tucked tight all around the bed. She beat me with an extension cord. She whacked my head, back, butt, and my legs with that extension cord. Oh, my goodness it hurt so badly! That's why I didn't want her to whip me again.

My mother never explained to me what I had done wrong. At nine years old, I was just having fun playing in the mud. I accidently peed in my panties and took them off so I could continue playing. One of my siblings told our mother that people were driving by in their cars looking under my dress. I didn't know I'd done anything wrong; I just wanted to take off my wet underwear. Wow! That whipping my mother gave me hurt so badly.

I prayed to God, " to let me die." Now I am very thankful that God didn't answer my prayer. Wow! I wouldn't be writing my story today. Oh, my goodness! My mother could give some whippings that really hurt. I was bleeding from the whelps on my body; however, the lesson I learned from that was to always to keep on my underwear. (LOL) Back to when Donnie and I ran away from home. The Police Officer drove us home. He said "Mrs. Beckman, I found your children. They were asleep a few miles away from home.

Our mother said, "Officer, "Since Donnie has asthma we'll keep him home. But you can take Nancy to Juvenile Hall. She does not obey me." I started crying. I was hoping my mother would give me another chance. That was my first time running away.

At 12, I didn't know how hard life could be by running away from home. I just focused on getting out of a whipping. Oh, how wrong I was. After, the officer took me away, I wished I had stayed home to take the whipping instead. The pain of being away from home was far worse. That was the only time I chose a whipping over leaving home. The police offer handcuffed me. My body was shaking. I was afraid because I didn't want to leave home. He tried to calm me down by telling me I'd be alright. He said the people at Juvenile Hall would be nice to me, and he drove me to there.

I thought about not seeing my family again. I started crying. Nobody loves me. I yelled and kicked the back of the passenger's seat in the patrol car. I cried telling the officer, "I'm not a bad girl. I cried louder. I know I'm not a bad girl." I began sobbing out of control, yelling at the Officer, "I'm not a bad girl. So the officer started the car and turned the siren on evidently to drown out the sound of my crying. He drove at a high speed hurrying to reach our destination. I was sliding back and forth on the back seat as he turned the corners. It was a very sad day for me. I didn't know why I had to leave home. I was so frightened. I sat in the back seat crying my heart out. That was the most terrifying day in my life.

Chapter 2

JUVENILE HALL

I cried every night until I went to sleep. I missed my family so much, I didn't eat my food. The Nurse asked the Judge to let me go back home. I was in Juvenile Hall for two weeks. The Judge reviewed my case, he asked, "Nancy, if I let you go home in two more days will you obey your parents?" Yes, Your Honor, I've learned my lesson. I won't run away from home again.

But my parents asked the judge to keep me longer. The Judge asked, "Mr. & Mrs. Beckham, why do you want Nancy serve a longer sentence?" "This is not the first time she's misbehaved." "Well, what has she done that's worse than running away from home?" The Judge asked. "She climbs out of the window after dark, we don't know where she goes. She stays out until after 11:00 p.m." When I punish her, after a month she'll sneak out again. If she stayed in Juvenile Hall for a while, I think she'd learn a lesson.

Then Judge sentenced me to 6 months to a girl's school. The Reform Institution for Girls was so far away from home, it frightened me. I started crying. It hurt so bad to be away from my family. I cried so hard it made me sick. I had knots in my stomach and my head was hurting. I had never been away from home. Early the next morning my probation officer and I started our trip to the Girl's School. It was a 342-mile-long trip. I was so far from home. There were so many curves on the highway that we drove around, it gave me motion sickness. We had to make so many stops to settle my upset stomach. She gave me 7 up and crackers, which made my stomach feel better, and then I could enjoy the scenery. The Girl's School was in Santa Rosa, California; that's a few hundred miles north of Sacramento.

We drove pass a lot of beautiful trees. In the distance, I could see the ocean. I felt lonely, helpless, and homesick because I knew I couldn't go back home. I made up my mind to be content by working on my behavior each day. We were finally on a road without curves and my stomach felt better. Thank God!

The female driver drove down a long road leading to the school. Finally, we were close enough to see the buildings behind a huge fence. She got out of the car to unlock a tall gate so we could drive up to the school. There was a 6-foot-high fence that surrounded the school. It was to keep the girls in, and it kept predators out. We drove down a long driveway with tree on both sides before we arrived at the main parking lot.

The building we entered had two huge doors leading to the main office. It felt creepy when I entered that building. I can never forget the admitting clerk when she smiled, she had two big buckteeth. She was so tall that I had to hold my head back to look up at her. She gave me a big smile. Then she asked me to have a seat on a nearby bench. While I sat there, I heard my probation officer tell the clerk, "Nancy is the youngest girl here. She is 12 years old. The only crime she committed was running away from home. Can you believe that?" The receptionist looked at me saying, "No, she's too young to be here." After I heard them say I was too young to be there. I was afraid and didn't know what could happen to me.

Chapter 3

GIRLS TRIED TO RAPE ME

Next, the security guard took me through a huge heavy metal door where we entered a building with bars on them. After I entered the room, I heard the metal door slam behind me with a loud sound. My heart was beating fast. I stood there terrified. I heard fast footsteps coming. I heard voices. They were chanting. We got fresh meat, ah, we got fresh meat. I was frightened. I was sitting on a bench, when five girls rushed toward me. They grabbed me and slammed me to the floor. I screamed at the top of my voice. Mama! Help me! Two girls were holding my shoulders down, one on each side, while two more girls held my legs wide open. The fifth girl was trying to shove an object inside me.

Before any harm came to me, I saw a bright light fill the room. Next, I felt a surge of energy permeate my whole body. The girls screamed, "Let's get out of here." I felt huge hands picking me up off the floor, and stood me up in the corner of the room. I never knew who it was that picked me up. Next, I noticed the five girls were fighting each other. They were screaming and punching each other. My fear of them had subsided. I didn't know then, why those things were happening to me.

The security guards had to stop the girls from fighting with me. I stood in the corner amazed watching the girls as they fought one another.

I didn't understand why they had stopped attacking me to fight each other. It was as clear as day when I began writing this story. God revealed it to me. The hands I felt lift me off the floor were my guardian angels. They rescued me from the girls. I realize it now; it was a divine intervention I had.

The girls had spread rumors about me. They told the other girls that I had super strength. They said, that I had fought off 5 girls single-handed. The girls asked me, how did I get so strong. I didn't know what they were talking about. They were the ones who attacked me. I was tired of telling them, I was the victim, not the attacker.

Chapter 3a - "The Battle Is Not Yours"

I learned to have faith in God when I was going through trials. He not only blessed me to recall all the things I went through but also He gave me an amazing mental picture of it. The memories brought tears to my eyes. I had mixed emotions of happiness and pain in my heart.

The mixed emotions I felt were when I realized that ELOHIM (God) had brought me through all those painful things. At the same time, I experienced tears of joy; I learned the battle is not ours, it's the LORD'S. Praise God, thank you Jesus for all you brought me through. To the readers I had to share this with you, I hope it strengthens your faith in God. The Bible says, "The battle is not ours; it's the LORD'S! That's Great News! Now that I'm a senior; I give my battles to the LORD because it's a spiritual warfare that we are in! Only God can conquer it for us.

Chapter 3b - Mrs. Miller Encouraged Me

It was my second day at the Girls Reform School, I knelt beside my bed to pray. I was thanking God for protecting me from the girls. We didn't have privacy in our rooms because there were no doors on them. I heard footsteps coming, and stop at my room. I opened my eyes to see who it was. A woman was standing there. With a big smile on her face, she said, "It's breakfast time, Kamiah." My name is Mrs. Miller and I am your day time supervisor this week.

When Mrs. Miller found me praying she said, "I'm so sorry for interrupting your prayer, Kamiah." "That's alright." She smiled at me. She reached out to hold my hand. Then she said, "Kamiah, I know you're not a bad girl. So how did you end up here?" I ran away from home because my parents were going to whip me, I answered. "What did you do to deserve a whipping?" She asked. "I took my younger brother with me to run away from home. We wanted to watch television 4 blocks away from home." She took her eyeglasses off while bugging her eyes. With her hand on her hip, her mouth flew open in disbelief.

"Aw, what a shame! you're too young to be here. You only disobeyed your mother, you didn't commit a crime. No, you're not a bad girl."

It made me happy that she believed in me. She made me feel important, I felt loved and she gave me hope.

When I was with my parents they never encouraged me like Mrs. Miller did. With my parents, I felt unloved because I always heard when I did something wrong. I never knew when I did anything right. Most of the time I didn't know I was doing anything wrong. Even when I did it. In those days parents whipped us without explaining what we did wrong.

After I became a parent, I learned a valuable lesson from my youngest son Jason. He was 6 years old when I spanked him for doing something wrong. He was smart enough to wait until I calmed down. Then he expressed his feelings to me. "Mom, why did you spank me before I even knew what I did wrong?" "If you warn me first, then if I do it again then you should spank me," he said. I had to agree with my son. He was speaking with wisdom. So I listened to him. I began giving him a warning whenever he did something wrong. I didn't know how to express my opinion when my parents disciplined me. But I changed the way I reared my children because my son was right.

My parents should have given me a warning first, then, if I ran away from home again I would expect a whipping. I believe I would've listened and obeyed them because I wanted to please them. No, that wasn't the case, it was my first time running away from home. My parents didn't allow me a second chance. They just sent me away to the girl's school. That's what hurt me so bad. On the other hand, Mrs. Miller gave me hope by telling me I was a good girl. She explained, "Kamiah if you stay out of trouble you can go home early." "Does that sound good to you?" As I smiled back at her, I said, I will be good I promise.

When she said, I was a good girl I felt like she cared about me. For the first time, I really felt like I had a friend that knew me. She always cheered me up. She said things to encourage me. While we were walking to the cafeteria, I saw the girls who tried to rape me. We lived in two separate dorms. When our group was passing by theirs, they were evading eye contact with me. They acted like they were afraid of me.

At the time, I didn't understand why the girls stopped fighting me to turn on each other? I felt sorry for them. I knew they couldn't blame me because I was standing in the corner of the room. I was watching them fight each other. I was confused.

I didn't know at the time in 1952, that angels were protecting me from those girls. We just changed the subject. "Kamiah when you were home with your parents did you go to church?" she asked. "Yes," I replied. "We went to a Seventh Day Adventist church, I added. Mrs. Miller said, "I am a Seventh Day Adventist also. "How would you like to go to church with me?" she asked. "Yes, I'd like to go." I was excited about going to church with her. At least I could get away from the bad girls, I thought.

Evidently, the girls had spread rumors about me; they were saying she's not the one to pick a fight with. They didn't understand that it wasn't me who attacked the girls. It was my angels who attacked the girls. The girls asked me a lot of questions I didn't have answers to. I sighed! I put my hands on my hips and stomped my foot on the ground and walked away. The girls were yelling across the campus asking me, "Did you really beat up the other girls by yourself?" "Why are you so strong?" I had no answers because I never touched the girls. They only thought I did. After, I ignored them they left me alone.

I was walking alone, I was wishing they'd leave me alone. I'm not the kind of person who likes to argue. So I stopped taking to them. They didn't believe it wasn't me who attacked them. I was 5 ft tall, and wore a size 6 dress. I was shorter and younger than all of them. At that time, I didn't know that it was my angels who protected me. It was on February 12, 2010 when I started typing this memoir. That's when God showed me how he protected me from the girls who tried to rape me. God is real! He sent His angels to protect me. Now that I'm an adult recalling the miracles that happened to me, it gives me tears of joy. I had to take a break from typing as tears streamed down my face. Just to know that God was fighting my battle for me. I am crying with tears of joy because I know now that God is with us even when we don't know it. Praise God, thank you Jesus.

After being there for a few weeks, all the girls were still insisting I beat up the girls all by myself. By then, I didn't argue with them. I let them believe what they thought happened. That way they wouldn't know how to deal with me. They'd just have to guess about me. Some of the girls were bragging and laughing about the crimes they had committed. One girl yelled out, "My boyfriend and I sold drugs." At 12, I didn't know what drugs were. My parents never let me socialize with other people.

As they yelled! some of the girls said they had stolen clothing.. The others said they were prostitutes. By telling their crimes, they were trying to get me to talk about the things I had done. I was done with them. The noise was getting out of hand. The supervisor blew the whistle for them to be quiet. The girls were quiet again. So I kept right on eating my lunch. I just ignored them. That's when the girls stopped asking me questions.

Chapter 4

FIRST CRIME COMMITTED AFTER INCARCERATION

Before we went to our classes, we returned to the dormitory. We picked up our book bags to take to our math class. It was my first day there. The teacher shook my hand and said, "Hello Kamiah, I'm Mrs. Sanders." I gave her my enrollment forms. With a smile, she said "Kamiah, you have a unique name. You are the first "Kamiah" I've met. I was shy because all the girls were giving me a mean look. They frowned at me like they didn't like me. I held my head down and said, "I guess so." The teacher shook my hand. She pointed to the desk in back row for me to sit.

I was at the Girl's School for six months. I stayed out of trouble all that time. The School Board called me into the office to give me a behavior progress test. I was behaving well I got along with the other students. They were considering releasing me to go home. Until one day while I was attending my math class. The girls were passing a note around in the classroom, it ended up in my hands. The math teacher Mrs. Sanders said, "Give me that note." The girls were whispering behind the teacher's back. I could see them. They were shaking their fist at me. They were gritting their teeth, as they whispered, "If you give her that note we'll kick your ass."

When the teacher tried to take the note from me, I stood up, I ran across the room to get away from her. Then the teacher said to me again, "Give me that note." The girls were yelling. "Don't do it." They were still shaking their fists at me. By that time the teacher walked over to her desk to open the drawer.

I didn't wait to see what she pulled out of the desk. I was afraid of the girls threatening to beat me up. Before I knew it, I grabbed the metal waste paper can. I hit her over the head with it. She screamed! Then she grabbed her bleeding head. The blood was all over her clothes too. She yelled, "Oh my God!" It frightened me so bad I couldn't move. The girls starred at me. They were bugging their eyes with their mouth opened in shock. They yelled at me. "Ooo! You're in trouble."

The teacher went back to her desk to sit down. She held the blood-soaked paper towels to her head. She called the office for help on the intercom. It didn't take long for the paramedics to get there. She was rushed to the hospital. I hid under the teacher's desk. It didn't take the guard very long to find me; the classroom was small. "Come on out!" he said.

I cried. I didn't mean to hurt her. I didn't mean to hurt her. Still sitting under the desk crying out of control. I really didn't mean to hurt Mrs. Sanders." I was hoping she didn't die. I was sorry that I hurt her. I didn't want the security guard to take me to detention. He wasn't at all sympathetic with me for crying. He reached under the desk, grabbed my arm and jerked me out. He tried to put handcuffs on me. He was unsuccessful and called for assistance. So we got a feisty little girl here." I kept pulling away from him. I kicked him.

Two more guards rushed in to assist him. They wrestled with me down to the floor like I was an adult. I had strength beyond my knowledge. I kicked them and socked them with my fist. I was like I was a boxer. It only made the situation worse. I fought with three officers. They called for three more officers to assist them. It took six adults to put me into the straightjacket.

They didn't have an easy job. I gave them a hard time. I kicked them, bit them, and screamed at the top of my voice. I was crying. I called out to Jesus. I'm sorry; I didn't mean to hurt her. I fought with the officers for a long time! I heard one of the officers say, "We need to give her an injection to calm her down." When they said they were going to give me an injection to calm me down. I stopped resisting.

Chapter 4a - Prayed For Forgiveness

After several hours in lockup, I heard a knock on the heavy metal door. "Tap, Tap, Tap. I saw the officer's face looking at me through a miniature window in the door. She said, "Kamiah I brought your dinner. That was good news to me." I was so hungry after I fought with the guards. After the officer came into my cell she said, "When I remove the straightjacket from you, will you behave yourself?" Yes, I responded. I thought about what if the teacher would've died. I prayed, and asked God to forgive me.

I cried myself to sleep. The days were going by slow, it seemed like I was in detention forever. I had nothing to do, so I read the Bible. I didn't understand it. But it was a good book for me to read. I was learning how I should live my life from the biblical stories and the Holy Spirit.

It was a hot summer afternoon. I was in detention. A few days had passed, a female psychiatrist gave me a visit and asked "Kamiah, you are so young, why are you here?" That was the first crime I ever did in my life. I only ran away from home. My parents sent me away to Juvenile Hall, next I ended up here. She asked, "Why did you hit your teacher on the head?" The girls threatened to beat me up if I gave the teacher the bad note. The teacher asked me to give it to her but I refused. It had bad words on it." The girls were going to beat me up. I was afraid of them.

"Tell me what did the note say?" She asked. "It said the teacher was a B-t-h." I began sobbing. "I didn't mean to hurt Mrs. Sanders. I want to go home!" At that time, the psychiatrist said to me, "Kamiah the only way you can go home, you'll have to be good." I cried so hard. I said, Mrs. Miller said I was a good girl.

The psychiatrist gave me a hug to comfort me. She said, "Stop crying. Listen I have something important to tell you." She took her hand off my shoulder and placed her hand on mine. Her other hand was under my chin to lift my head to get eye contact. She paused to give me a stern look. She said "I know you are a good girl. But you allowed the devil's spirit to control you. "Do you understand what I am telling you?" Yes, when I was at home, my parents taught me that people are bad because they listen to the Devil. After that, the psychiatrist said that I'd be alright. She said, "Now that we are friends, I'll come visit you once a month."

Chapter 4b - My Teacher Forgave Me

Mrs. Sanders came to visit me while I was in detention. Her head was still wrapped in bandages. I felt sad that I had caused her injury. I was glad that she was doing better. When I saw her, I was relieved to know that she was still alive! She gave me a great big hug and said to me, "Kamiah, I know you're not a bad girl, Okay!"

I held my head down looking at the floor. I felt unworthy of her kindness. Mrs. Sanders held her hand under my chin and gently raised my head so we could have eye contact. She said, "Kamiah I love you, and I forgive you." When she said she loved me and forgave me too, it felt like a ton of weight lifted off my shoulders. I really felt like she cared about me. Mrs. Sanders asked me to have lunch with her in the staff's lounge. Mrs. Sanders said, she had forgiven me for hurting her. She made me feel special. I was happy to accept her invitation.

I ordered my favorite food: a hamburger, French fries, and a Pepsi cola to drink, it was so delicious. It had been a long time since I had a burger and fries. I was swinging my feet under the table as I enjoyed my meal. While eating our lunch, Mrs. Sanders smiled, she said," I wish you were my little girl! I never had children.

Wow! She really made me feel special. It was cruel that I hurt her for no reason. It was hard for me to understand why she forgave me. "Kamiah, what would you like to be when you grow up?" She asked. I had to think for a minute. "Oh, I'd like to be a teacher." I replied. "What is it that you like about a teaching?" "I like getting dressed in beautiful clothes, and have a key to my classroom." I had a lot of fun talking to Mrs. Sanders. That was the first time I laughed and talked with an adult. "Kamiah do you mind telling me about your family?" I don't mind. I have seven sisters and five brothers. "I am amazed that you came from such a large family. That's wonderful," she responded.

She sat back in the cushy chair with a smile on her face. I felt comfortable talking with her. She told me about when she was a little girl. How she played with rag dolls. She pretended that they were her children. We enjoyed our time together so much. It was the best conversation I ever had with an adult! When I didn't know how to pronounce a word, she would say it and spell it for me. She seemed like she really enjoyed listening to me. When I'd talk to her, she would have a big smile on her face. Before that day I thought that no one cared about me.

When I was at home, my parents would give me whippings every day. They never told me when I did anything right. They always told me when I did something wrong. Mrs. Sanders asked, "Did your parents have talks with you about life? No, the only conversations I've had were with my siblings when we played games.

She asked, "Have you ever talked with your mother about personal problems?" I looked down at my folded hands with tears in my eyes. No. She handed me a Kleenex tissue. "Now, I understand you never knew how to speak up for yourself when the girls bullied you." That's why you didn't tell the teacher you didn't write the note. She smiled while talking to me so kindly. I didn't know how to express myself. I was so sad. I sat there wiping tears from my eyes.

Mrs. Sanders gave me a lot of quality time. It really touched my heart. It gave me a reason to want to be a better person. She gave me hope, showed me love, and forgave me. My teacher was the best teacher I ever had. She understood that I had some deep issues I didn't even understand. She was more than just an academic teacher. She taught me how to forgive others. Mrs. Sanders was a 5 ft 4" tall Caucasian woman. Her hair was auburn with a touch of gray in it. She looked to be in her late forties or early fifties.

She gave me hope by forgiving me. I felt like I could accomplish anything after that. When she forgave me, she taught me by her example; that when others hurt me, I need to forgive them. Once, I got angry at someone when they hurt me. When I didn't forgive them, it caused me to have diarrhea. After I forgave them, my diarrhea ceased right away. I was 16 at that time. From that day on I decided to get over anger in a hurry. I learned to forgive people right away.

Mrs. Sanders reminded me to always choose to do the right thing, instead of doing wrong. She said, never let others lead me astray. I told her that I was sorry for hurting her. She gave me a big hug. I cried because I was ashamed of myself. Because of that, I learned to never do wrong because of peer pressure.

Chapter 5

SEDUCED BY HOMOSEXUAL

After dinner, we went back to our dormitories. That night we could stay up late to decorate for the holiday. I rushed to my room to finish drawing a picture. I wanted to surprise Mrs. Miller with it before she went home for the weekend. She was so nice to me. It was getting close to Christmas. We were excited because it was time for us to exchange gifts.

I saw a girl across the room, who was watching my every move. I asked the girl who was sitting next to me named Julie, "What's that girl's name that keeps watching me?" "Oh! That's Billy," she replied. She went on to describe her. She said, "Kamiah, is that the girl you we are sitting by Mrs. Sander?"

Yes. I pointed to the dark-skinned girl with her hair cut short. Yes, she's the one. "Is she the same girl, who walks with a limp in her leg? Julie said. "Yes, we're talking about the same person!"

Billy weighed 150 lbs, and she was about 4ft 5" tall. I'd never seen her before. I noticed she was watching me as I walked around the gymnasium room. I was on my way to my bedroom. I met with Julie again. She is an Italian and about 5ft 5" tall. I asked, "How long has Billy been here at the school?" "Billy has been here over a year!" She replied. Billy had been serving time in lockup because she had a fight with the life guard. She broke her arm. "She got detention for six months, that's the reason you haven't seen her since you've been here.

I headed toward my room, once again. Before I entered my room, I took one last look to see if Billy was still watching me. Sure enough, she was still looking at me. I didn't think any more about her looking at me. So I just went into my room, and lay on my twin size bed. I was tired. On school nights, we had to go to bed at 9:00 O'clock. It was the Christmas weekend. This night we got to stay up until 11:00. I was so sleepy. I fell asleep shortly after laying on the bed.

Billy startled me out of my sleep when she leaned over me. She put her hand over my mouth to keep me quiet. She whispered, "Be quiet, I'm not going to hurt you. I'm going to show you a good time." Our rooms didn't have doors, so, she could walk right in. I was shocked when I woke up. She said she only wanted to talk to me. I relaxed a moment just to hear what she had to say.

Billy looked like a guy, but she was a sixteen-year-old girl. She had dark brown eyes with thick eyebrows. Her nose was flat and wide. Her bottom lip was larger than the top. She talked with a lisp (speech difficulty.) When she walked, she'd limp on one leg. So as I had mentioned earlier, Billy said she just wanted to show me a good time. I didn't know what she was talking about. I asked, "What do you mean a good time?" At that time, she pulled the covers off me. Then she climbed into the bed with me. I pushed her. Wait a minute. Get away from me. It was about 12:00 midnight.

I yelled. Get Billy out of my room. I was still a virgin, that was the first time someone touched me on my private parts. The guard and supervisor rushed to my room. They got there before she could get away. "What did she do to you?" The guard asked. She touched my vagina. She had violated my rights. So the guard handcuffed her, and took her to detention. I found out that she was a lesbian. That was my first time I heard of a homosexual. I didn't even know what sex meant. I never knew that girls liked to kiss other girls I thought, that is so sickening, yuck. I only saw men and women kiss when I was a young girl. It really disturbed me to hear that girls kissed each other!

It was 12:30 that morning, when the guard took Billy to detention. I couldn't go back to sleep. So the last time I looked at the clock it was 1:15a.m. I over slept when it was time to go to breakfast the next morning. The supervisor came to wake me. I brushed my teeth and got dressed in a hurry, but I forgot to comb. When we got to the cafeteria, I heard the girls were talking about how I got Billy in trouble…they said, she was back in detention.

Chapter 5a - Church With Mrs. Miller

When Mrs. Miller arrived on her morning shift, the girls told her that they heard Billy came into my room at midnight. Mrs. Miller was the day supervisor. She asked to speak to me before I went to volleyball practice. She said, "There are rumors going around the campus that you got Billy locked up last night." "Yes, that's true," "What happened, Kamiah?" I explained, "Billy was in my room, and got into my bed trying to seduce me. I yelled for help. The security guard came to my room and took Billy detention last night.

Mrs. Miller said, "Kamiah I'm glad you're staying out of trouble!" A week after Billy tried to molest me, Mrs. Miller invited me to go to church with her. She said I could spend weekends with her. "Are you ready to go to church with me now?" She asked. Yes, I am. "The Administration Board approved for you to spend the weekend with me. Would you like that?" Yes! I answered. She took me shopping with her. She bought me some beautiful dresses to wear to church. Wow! I was excited. It seemed like it was a dream to me that Mrs. Miller was so nice. Nobody I ever met had been so nice to me like Mrs. Miller.

On Friday, she left work early to buy me some church clothes; we went to the shopping center in downtown Santa Rosa. We passed by a farm home which had a pond with ducks swimming in front of it. I said, "Oh! That's beautiful!" Mrs. Miller said, "Yes, it is, Kamiah! She made me feel so special when we talked. She was always interest in what I had to say. But I never talked with my mother like that.

It took us 30 minutes to get to the Santa Rosa shopping center. We parked in front of a nice large department store. The store had plenty of beautiful dresses for little girls. It was difficult to decide on which dress to pick. She let me buy two dresses. One dress was yellow with ruffles trimmed on the sleeves and at the bottom. The other dress was lavender it had ruffles around the collar and at the bottom. Next, we went to the shoe store next door. She bought me one pair of white patent leather shoes and two pairs of white sox with dainty ruffles on them. We had one more stop to make at the market.

I enjoyed being with Mrs. Miller, she treated me like I was her daughter. I thanked her for buying the nice clothes for me, and gave her a big hug. She said, "Kamiah I'm glad you're happy." Finally, we arrived at her two stories home. Her husband came to greet us. She showed me the room upstairs where I'd be sleeping.

Later, after dinner, she showed me the rest of the house. It was the most beautiful home I'd ever seen. After we ate, she invited me to join them in the living room. We sang gospel songs while she played the piano. We read Bible Scriptures and had prayer to close out the worship service before we went to bed. Saturday morning, we got ready for church. The church was so huge, it had the tallest steeple I've ever seen!

The people were so friendly to me. After church, we ate a delicious dinner. It was a variety of foods to choose from.

The people came over to shake my hand and some of them gave me hugs. They were very friendly.

The members asked me to come visit them again. I had a wonderful time with Mrs. Miller that weekend. I really wasn't ready to go back to the girl's school. When I saw the girls again they were asking me questions, "What did you do?" "Where did you go?" "What did Mrs. Miller's house look like?" I told them just as I described in my story, the girls said that they wished that they could go places outside of the school like me.

I was the only girl there that was a Seventh Day Adventist. That's the reason why I got to spend the weekend with Mrs. Miller. She told the girls that we go to church on Saturday and the Protestants have church on Sunday. She explained that the Protestant church groups come to the girls

School every Sunday, but the Seven Day Adventist does not come to the girl's school.

When I went to church with her off campus the girls wanted an excuse to leave the school too. I told Mrs. Miller how much I enjoyed spending the weekend with her. I was so happy to get away from the girl's school. So after that she invited me to join her every weekend.

Chapter 5b - Billy's Dorm Transfer

It was April 1953, it was a beautiful sunny spring day with blossoms on the fruit trees. I was going to my sewing class, when Mrs. Miller met me along the way. "Kamiah, I have good news for you." The guard moved Billy to another dorm. She has a restraining ordered to stay away you. I was so happy to know that.

Mrs. Miller said, "Kamiah, your sewing instructor has a package for you. I went to the class to claim it. My Uncle had bought some material for me. I was excited that I could complete my skirt. I had made a matching vest out of the beige corduroy material first. Mrs. Davis, the sewing teacher helped me to cut out my pattern. I finished my skirt set. Just before class was over the office clerk called to tell that I had visitors in the waiting room!

Chapter 6

PARENTS VISIT ME

I left the classroom in a hurry to get to the office. I was happy that someone came to see me. As soon as I walked into the administration office the Clerk said, "Kamiah you have visitors." Wow! when she said my parents were there, I jumped up and down all the way to the waiting room. When they sent me away to the girl's school, I never expected to see them again. My eyes got so big, I yelled out, Momma and daddy.

I didn't realize they loved me until they came to visit me. I was so happy they came. They brought my three-month-old baby sister with them. It was my first time seeing her. She was family member number fourteen. She let me hold my baby sister. She was so beautiful. When she smiled her cute little dimples showed.

My parents could stay with me longer when the staff served us lunch and dinner. My parents had asked my supervisor that whether my behavior had improved since? She told them that I had improved 100%. She added, that I was doing so well that in three months I'd be going home.

After their discussion, my parents gave me a big hug me before leaving. I cried! I didn't want to see them to go. My mother said, "If it's the Lord's will, we'll be back to visit you again." I smiled at my parents, and gave them one last hug. They were on their way out of the corridor, I watched them until they were out of sight.

When I went back to the dormitory, the girls heard that my parents came to visit me. They said they were so happy for me. Some of the girls never had a visitor, those who were there longer than me. When my parents came to visit me, it let me know that they loved me. It helped boost my self-esteem. I decided to stay away from the girl that were trouble makers.

I signed up for the swimming classes, and the tract team, so I could stay busy.

I thought to myself, I might as well enjoy the rest of my stay until they released me. When I returned to the dormitory, Mrs. Miller had left for the day. The evening supervisor Ms. Davis was on duty. She told me, "Before Mrs. Miller went home, she told me that your parents came to visit you. I'm happy for you."

"My parents brought my 3-month-old sister, I got to hold her!" "How many brothers and sisters do you have?" The supervisor asked. I counted my fingers, as I named them. I have five brothers, and now with my baby sister I have eight sisters. Her mouth flew open. She said, "My goodness you don't need friends to play with, you have plenty of friend's right at home.

Chapter 6a - Going Home

As the days passed, I marked off the remaining days from my calendar. I didn't have much time left before going home. It was August 1954, I missed my monthly period for 3 months when I was age 14. It was time for me to go before the board meeting for them to review my behavior record. It showed that I had improved one hundred percent. The staff members congratulated me. I had two weeks before going home. "Wow! I was so excited, I jumped up and down. I told them thank you for teaching me so many things. They encouraged me by saying, "If you continue to be good, finish your education and you will do well in life."

The staff members shook my hand, hugged me, and we said our goodbyes. When I returned to the dormitory, Mrs. Miller was on duty. She greeted me "Hello Kamiah, I heard your parents were here to visit. I am so happy for you." "Thank you, Mrs. Miller, my parents brought my baby sister too." I said, she's so beautiful with cute little dimples just like my dad. With the biggest grin on my face.

I said "Mrs. Miller, I got good news. I'm going home in two weeks." "Great for you!" she said. "See Kamiah, I knew you could be good. Just ask God for help, you can be whatever you want to be it's up to you. Those valuable words still ring in my mind because Mrs. Miller was a caring person.

The staff surprised me before going home, ty let me They hired me to work in the office. I learned how to answer the telephone. It made me feel like an adult. I just felt great for the first time in my life. On my last day, they paid me $40.00 cash. The staff said, the money was an incentive for me to get a job after I finished going to school. I forgot to mention, the girls taught me how to smoke cigarettes too. But I am not proud of it. I smoked cigarettes from age 13 until I was 34. I thank God I quit smoking 45 years ago. For that, I give God the glory.

The day came for me to go home. My probation officer signed my release forms for me to go home. I was there for 18 months. It seemed like it was forever, It was August of 1954, I was 14. I was no longer the same innocent 12-year-old girl when I came to the institution. When I injured the school teacher Mrs. Sanders; I'm not proud that I committed that crime!

I kept thinking about what Mrs. Miller said. "You can be whatever you want to be with God's help." She told me to think first before doing something. While it was fresh on my mind, I repeated her words over and over in my mind. I wanted to be a better person when I went back home.

Mrs. Miller came to work an hour early on the day I was going home. She said he had to be there to hug me goodbye. I was already up and dressed. After Mrs. Miller arrived, she came to my room with a light tan suitcase she said, "Kamiah, it's for you, and here are your church clothes. I thanked her for the clothes and suitcase. "You can wear one of the dresses home if you'd like. She suggested. "Yes, that's a great idea." I hurried to my bedroom to change my clothes. I wore the lavender colored dress and the white patent leather shoes. Mrs. Miller said, "Kamiah you look beautiful!" I gave her a great big hug for treating me so special. I'll always remember Mrs. Miller. She was so kind to me. She encouraged me when I didn't feel like I was a good person.

With sympathy she said, "Why are you crying?" Before I answered her, I felt so bad, I kept crying. I was so ashamed it was hard for me to talk. Between words, I had to take a long breath. Mrs. – Miller, you're – the only one – who showed me – that you care – about me, "Sweetheart there are other people who love and care about you, but they have a different way of showing it. "For example, Kamiah parents do their best providing basic needs for their children. They may forget to give them quality time, but it doesn't mean they don't love you. After Mrs. Miller gave me good advice we gave each other a big hug. Then I was on my way out of the front door waving goodbye to her.

Chapter 6b - Wow! Going Home

Mrs. Miller told me that all people don't express their love for each other in the same way. After I had children I realized being a parent is not easy. That showed me that my parents did love me by the way they provided for me. After that, I stopped comparing my parents with others to how they showed their love for me.

While I was at the girl's school I learned office procedures which prepared me for employment. It was my last day to complete the office skills class. My Probation Officer and I met for the first time. She was a tall lady! She leaned down to look at me and smiled as she said, "I'm taking you home."

It made the time go by fast by working in the office before going home. She asked, "Do you want to be a clerical employee when you grow up?" Yes, I'd like to work in an office like this one. It was fun! But I was more excited to be going home to see my family.

I was so happy after we left the office. It seemed like it was a dream to be going home. Marilyn and I waited in the car a few minutes while she looked at the map. She said, "Kamiah, I see from your record your parents moved to another town since you came here." I asked, what is their new address? Your parents moved to 1015 Oakwood Avenue, Venice, California." "Well it looks like I'll be taking you to your new home in Venice. Are you excited?" Wow! Yes, I'm just happy to be going home.

We started on our journey seven O'clock that morning. It was so exciting to be going home. I was bouncing up and down on the front seat of the car. I looked out of the car window to take a last look at the place I stayed for 18 months. There were sheep grazing on the green hillsides. I saw the fruit trees filled with fruit too. It was so beautiful!

We drove on the highway for two hours, by that time I was hungry. I didn't have an appetite before we left, so I didn't eat breakfast. We stopped to eat at a café on the highway. I ordered a hamburger with Thousand Island dressing: lettuce, onions, dill pickles, and tomatoes; with hot crispy golden-brown French fries. I also had an icy cold Pepsi cola drink. It was so delicious.

It had been a long time since I had a hamburger. After I ate, I was stuffed. In a few minutes, I felt sleepy. The next thing I knew Marilyn woke me up for a restroom break. We still had a long way to go before getting home. I stretched and yawned, as I rubbed my eyes. I looked out the window trying to figure out what city we were passing through.

I saw a sign on the highway, it was Fresno! I knew it wasn't too far from Bakersfield! When we got to the downtown area of Fresno we had a 15-minute rest break. She bought me a delicious Frosty Freeze ice cream cone. It had hot chocolate and chopped walnuts on top. Yummy, it was good!

She turned the car radio on it was playing gospel songs. I really enjoyed it. At the girl's school, we only heard Country Western music to listen to. It was my first time going to Venice, and I didn't know how long it would take to get there.

While driving through the mountains we saw another sign posted for 60 miles to Los Angeles. I was in the back seat lying down. "Well it won't be long before we get to Venice," Marilyn said. I sat up to look out the window, I started bouncing up and down in the back seat saying, "Whoopi! At last, we were arriving in Los Angeles. Marilyn stopped at a service station to call my parents at a phone booth. My mother was at home. So she got the directions and landmarks to my parent's home.

We finally arrived in Venice. I was excited to see what it looked like. It was my first time there. It didn't take us long to find our way around Venice. It was a small town. We parked drove up to their white house painted with forest green trimmed around the windows, the porch, and the roof top. Yes, we were at the correct address: 1015 Oakwood Avenue.

I saw my mother waiting on the front porch holding my baby sister. I jumped out the car and ran to meet them. I wrapped my arms around both together. My mother invited my Probation Officer to stay for dinner with us. "No thank you, Mrs. Beckman your daughter and I just finished dinner. I made sure Kamiah didn't come home hungry." She replied. "Thank you, for feeding my daughter." "You're welcome Mrs. Beckman."

I'll keep in touch with you to follow up on Nancy. I must hurry now; I have another appointment to go to. She gave my mother her business card. We walked her to the car. I thanked Marilyn for bringing me home to my family. I gave her a big hug. Then we waved goodbye as she drove away.

It was August 1954, school was out for the summer. I was glad to be home with my siblings. My father who was a jolly daddy had just come in from work. It was 5:00 that evening. He said "Good-Night! Girl, you sure have changed. You look like a young lady now." Then he gave me a big hug. My father was excited; he'd express himself by saying, "Good night!" When he said, "good night," with a deep sound coming from his belly that meant it was from his heart.

Chapter 6c - Sisters Talked All Night

It was a warm Monday evening in August 1954, I was age 14. It was my first day home from the Girls school. My family members asked me a lot of questions about the school; we talked and laughed until bedtime. My sister Venetia showed me to her bedroom. We shared a bed together. It was so many of us, we all had to share a bed. Venetia was 16 years old. At our ages, we acted like young ladies. We wore high heels shoes and makeup.

I learned a lot of things from the girl's school. Venetia and I talked all night about girl stuff. Our bedroom was right next to our parent's bedroom. Our mother knocked on the wall. "Alright you girls stop that noise and get to sleep." My sister and I got quiet for a minute, and then we started giggling and whispering again. It was 1:00 in the morning, we were still talking.

Chapter 7

HOMOSEXUAL SEEKS REVENGE

The weather was chilly, it was the end of October 1954. I'd been home for two months from the Girl's School. It was Halloween night. There was a big party going on at the community center. It was a block away from home. I asked my mother if I could go to the party. She said, "Only if you get your chores done." So I put on my best behavior. I did my chores. I also baked a chocolate cake for my mother. It's her favorite dessert.

The aroma of the cake filled the air and it looked good too. By showing her, I could cook, then she'd let me go to the party. After dinner, everybody had a slice of cake with vanilla ice cream. They smacked their lips. They were saying how delicious it tasted.

An hour later, after they ate their dessert everybody was moaning and holding their head. They were saying, they had a headache. My mother said, "How much Crisco oil did you put in the cake?" I answered, "I poured two cups of Crisco oil in the cake." "I thought you knew how to bake a cake." My father said, "Good night girl! Don't cook anything else until you learn how to cook." LOL Daddy I'm sorry! I thought I was baking it right. I didn't cook anything else after that. That was alright with me, because I had older sisters who knew how to cook. I was just trying to impress my mother so I could go to the Halloween party.

It was a few days before the Halloween party started. I'd been doing well at home. I got permission from my parents to go to the party. I was glad I could to the party with Venetia and my brother Gregory. I was 14, and never had been to a party. My brother was 4 years older than me. He let me wear his big baggy clothes so, I could dress up as a bum for the party! I had a rag tied around my head, and wore his big shoes too! I also carried a mop stick with a bundle of rags tied around it. We all had on homemade costume! We looked so funny!

The recreation center was a half a block away from our house. Before we left home, our mother gave us instructions to come home as soon as the party was over. We assured her we'd come home right away. The Recreation Center was so close to our house we could hear the music playing before we got there! It was Diana Ross and The Supremes! As we entered the party the room was dim with blue lights!

There was a crowd of people dancing. I was having fun with my brother and sister showing me the latest dance steps! This was my first dance party. When the Latin Music played, I showed my siblings how to do the dance the mambo. I learned it at the Girls School.

While we were having a good time dancing. I felt someone tap me on the shoulder. I turned around to see the person in dismay. It was Billie, the lesbian, that tried to seduce me. She said, "I told you I'd find you." She came to get revenge because I had her locked up. I was so frightened, I yelled for my brother and sister to let's go home.

"What's wrong?" "I'll tell you on the way home." We had to run fast because Billie was chasing us.

Billie promised she'd get even with me. She kept her word. I had no idea how she knew where I lived. I never told her. I let my brother know that she was a lesbian, and that she came there to harm me.

As we ran home we looked back, but she couldn't run fast. She had a limp, but she continued to follow us. We reached our house just in time to lock the door. My brother secured the door by pushing the sofa against it. After a few minutes, she knocked on the door. My mother asked, "Who is it?" I heard her say, "I brought Kamiah a gift." "Don't believe her because she came to fight me." I explained.

My mother left the front door just in time. A brick came crashing through the glass window. Billy put her hand through the broken window to unlock the door. I ran out the back door. I yelled! Mrs. Chavez. "Call the Police! A crazy girl is chasing me." In the meantime, I stayed at our neighbor's house. Later, I found out that Billy had entered my parent's house. My brother Gregory hit her upside the head with the back of his gun.

The police officer asked me, "Why was she coming to hurt you?" Because she was going to molest me. So the guard locked her up in detention. After we were released from the girl's school, she said she would find me, and get revenge."

"So, she did find me." The police officer asked her, "Are those allegations against you true?" "It's true?" The Officer asked, "How was Billy's head injured?" I don't know I was at the neighbor's house. My brother Gregory said, "Officer I had to hit her; she tried to hurt my sister, Nancy."

The police officer asked Gregory, "Why did she try to hurt your sister?" Officer, "My sister will have to tell the reason why she's trying to hurt her I don't know. The Officer asked Gregory, "What did you use to hit Billie with?" He answered, "I hit her with the back end of my gun." "Was the gun loaded?" "No Sir."

The officer booked Billy, then she was taken to jail. My mother and I filed a restraining order against her the next day. I didn't have to worry about her bothering me.

Our lives were getting back to normal, after Billy was in Jail. It was two months before Christmas Day. We asked our older brother to buy the Christmas lights for us to decorate the house. We wanted to surprise our parents.

Our parents went to shop for our gifts for us. So Venetia, Gregory, and I had to decorate the house with the Christmas lights while they were gone. When our parents returned home, they saw the Christmas light. They were shocked because we surprised them. They said we did a good job decorating the house. It was fun decorating the house and singing Christmas songs. Christmas was an exciting time of the year for us. After opening the gifts, we had plenty of delicious food to eat. Even though we had turkey and stuffing for Thanksgiving Day, my mother would cook the same dinner for Christmas as well. We would change a few side dishes to make it a little different for Christmas. We'd have turnip greens, cornbread stuffing, cranberry sauce, and potato salad for Thanksgiving Day. But for Christmas, we'd have green beans, corn on the cob, and cornbread stuffing with turkey and cranberry sauce. We always had sweet potato pie and German chocolate cake. It was another favorite for the holiday dinner. Yummy!

The week before New Year's we got to ride the one bicycle which we had to share with 8 siblings. The four younger siblings were not big enough to ride the bike.

I didn't like to celebrate New Year's Eve, because it was too noisy. The people shot guns in the air. It frightened me. It was January 1955, there was frost on the ground. It looked beautiful, but it was cold outside. Our new Christmas coats really came in handy. The holidays were over. It was time to go back to school. It was hard to get out of my warm bed on those cold winter mornings.

In those days, we had real winters. There was snow on the ground. We'd go outside to make snowmen and throw the snowballs at each other. It was so much fun. Springtime was when we enjoyed looking at the fruit trees in bloom. The weather was just right in the 1960s and 1970s. The summers were nice and warm, not too hot, but just right. It was a lot of fun to go to the beach then. We took a picnic lunch to the beach. We had our beach towels, and a beach ball to have fun with.

Chapter 7a - Avoiding Discipline

It was February 1, 1955, it was so nice to be home with my family again. I was ready to go back to school. I had finished my laundry by hand and hung the clothes on the line. I had monthly cramps and had to go to bed. I cuddled under the blankets with a heating pad on my stomach and fell asleep.

When I woke up, I heard my mother fussing at my sister Venetia. "Why did you leave dirty dishes in the sink?" "Mother, it was Nancy's turn to clean up the kitchen. I cleaned it yesterday!" Venetia replied, "Mother, she said, for the last month, I've been cleaning up the kitchen even when it was Nancy's turn!" But I'm tired of cleaning up on her days!" Our mother yelled at me. "Nancy when your father comes home; you're gettin a whippin!"

Chapter 8

Married A Stranger

It was a winter night in February of 1955, the fog was so thick I couldn't see my hand before my face. I walked slowly because I couldn't see very far. I couldn't read the street signs until I stood right next to them. I ran away from home at the age of 14. In four more months, it would be my fifteenth birthday!

While I was walking in the fog, I bumped into a yellow fire plug on the sidewalk! I sat on it, not knowing where on earth I was going.! I had no friends. I was afraid to return home.

I sat there feeling lost and afraid of the dark. A few minutes went by, and I saw car's lights headed in my direction. The car stopped right where I was sitting. The fog lifted just enough that I could see it was a man in the car. He rolled down the window. He said, "Little girl what are you doing out here in the fog?" I don't know, I hunched my shoulders (It meant I didn't know.). I just looked down at the ground. "You don't have to sit there in the fog. Come sit in the car with me, I won't bite you." I sat there on the fire plug a few more seconds. Then he said, "Don't' you know it's dangerous out there?"

He leaned over in the car to swing the door wide open on the passenger's side. He patted his hand on the seat and said, "Come on, sit with me. It's cold out there." With a big smile he said, "Let's talk." I thought, I have nothing to lose. I didn't know where I was going anyway. So I got into his car.

He introduced himself to me. He leaned closer to me. He placed his hand on mine. "My name is Harold Gibbon, what's your name?" I was so shy. So I spoke softly. My name is Nancy. "Do you have a middle name?"

he asked. I looked down before I answered, because I was bashful. "Yes, I do." "My middle name is "Kamiah." "I really like your middle name. Do you mind if I call you Kamiah?" It impressed me that he liked my middle name. I agreed, that he could call me Kamiah. He said, "You can call me Harold. We'll both use our middle names. Is that okay with you?" Yes, that's fine with me.

Chapter 8a - First Dinner Together

I felt comfortable being in his company. He asked, "Would you like to join me for dinner?" Wow! He didn't know it, but he had just said the magic word because I was starving. "Kamiah, you never told me where you were going?"

"I don't know where I'm going because I'm running away from home." "Would you like to come and stay with me?" "Yes, I'd like to stay with you." "Okay, we'll go get something to eat. There are two nice restaurants down the street. They have Seafood and Mexican food.

I said, wow! I'd like to go to the Seafood Restaurant. We had fried shrimp, fried fish, coleslaw, and crispy golden-brown French fries along with the condiments; I mixed ketchup, hot sauce together. I topped it off with a Pepsi cola to drink.

He drove his brand new 1955 Chevy, I complimented on how beautiful it was! It was light-green with shiny chrome bumpers and tire rims. He said, "I just bought it a month before I met you. "Babe, last month I just came home from the military, and now I meet you. He didn't live far from the restaurant. We ordered our food to go. We went to his bachelor apartment to eat our dinner. I still had on the layers of clothing I wore when I left home. After he turned on the furnace, I was getting too warm. I excused myself to go to the bathroom. I took off all those clothes, except for one garment. I folded them and left them in the bathroom.

When I came out of the bathroom he was popping some popcorn. He said, "Babe come on let's watch the Amos and Andy show." He had a big bowl of popcorn on the coffee table. He also had a two glass of wine there. We snacked on popcorn, and sipped on the wine. That was my first-time drinking wine. I was feeling dizzy. So I leaned over to lay my head on his shoulder. I was so comfortable I went to sleep. When I woke up the Amos and Andy show was off.

He was watching a Cowboy and Indian movie when I woke up. He said, "Babe I'll let you sleep, you need to get some rest." I didn't talk very much, so, I sat there quiet. He said "Babe, before you went to the bathroom you looked a bit fatter, but when you came back, you look thinner. What happened?

All the clothing I had I wore on my body, instead of packing a suit case. I explained. By wearing all my clothes, my parents didn't know that I was running away from home. He asked, "Why did you run away from home?" After I finished doing my laundry, I wasn't feeling good. I had monthly cramps. My mother never asked why I didn't do the dishes. She just told my father I wasn't doing my share of chores around the house. My father was going to whip me. "I didn't want a whipping that's why I ran away from home.

"Did your parents know you were sick? "He asked. "Yes, I told my mother that I had monthly cramps and didn't feel good." But my father was going to whip me anyhow. "How does your stomach feel now?" "I still have cramps." We were sitting in the living room on the sofa bed. He went to the kitchen to get me a glass of warm water mixed with whiskey. After I drank the warm water with whiskey I felt better.

After I got tipsy he said, "Come on Babe let's dance." He had some 45 records and 78 albums from his oldie but goodies collection that he played. We had so much fun because I liked to dance.

We danced to a fast song by Bobby Blue Bland entitled "Honey Child"; another song by Mary Wells, "My Guy," and he played a song by the Platter's, "Only You." That's when he turned the lights down low as we danced. After the song was over he knelt on one knee. While holding my hand he asked, "Kamiah will you marry me?" Yes! He had been so nice to me since the moment we met. He was the first man in my life.

He was handsome with a neat-shaped mustache and nice broad shoulders. He wore his hair processed with finger waves. The cologne he wore smelled so good! I was so impressed, when he proposed to me because we had just met. I asked, "How old are you? "21," he replied. As he smiled at me he said, "Oh yes, I forgot to ask how old are you!" I answered, I'm 14. He said to me "If age doesn't matter to you, it doesn't matter to me."

Then we kissed for the first time. I wasn't worried about his age because I didn't want to go back home. When it was time to go to bed, I realized I didn't have a nightgown to sleep in. So he let me wear one of his extra-large T-shirts. It fit down below my knees.

The next day we went shopping to buy a nightgown and a wedding gown. He brought back two wine glasses with a bottle of red wine from the kitchen. We sat on the black leather sofa bed in the living room. After he poured the wine, we did a toast by touching our wine glasses together. He put a peppermint candy in his mouth, drew me closer to him for a kiss. As I lay in his arms on the bed he said, "Baby you are an angel. You were sent from heaven." When I was 11 years old, my mother told me, if a man kissed me, I would get pregnant. I was waiting for my stomach to get big after he kissed me. (LOL) He was the only person who had kissed me.

We didn't have sexual intercourse because I was on my monthly period. All I thought about after he kissed me was whether I got pregnant. I laid beside him on his arm. That was the first time I had an alcoholic drink too. I was drowsy and had fallen asleep in his arms. I woke up the next morning with a headache. I thanked God that I met a gentleman who took good care of me.

He went to the drug store to purchase a hot water bottle for me. I fell asleep. After I woke up, he asked, "Baby did you sleep good?" Yes, I sure did. Since I didn't know how to cook, we ate corn flakes with vanilla ice cream cones crushed into the cornflakes cereal with milk. That was his favorite breakfast. After breakfast, he called his job and asked to take off. He wanted to make sure we had groceries in the house before he went to work.

He asked, "Baby do you know how to cook?" I laughed, "No, I don't know how to cook!" One day I cooked a chocolate cake for my family. Everybody got a headache because I had put too much Crisco oil in the cake mix." "Baby that's okay, I'll just buy you some TV dinners." "We're going shopping today to buy food and some clothes for you.

Chapter 8b - Getting Married

We made it home after a long day of shopping, but I had fun buying clothes. My stomach was cramping again this time, he gave me a hot oil massage. It helped me feel better. Since we were going away for the weekend, he suggested I rest and take it easy. He put the groceries away, while I laid down on the sofa bed. He said, "Baby, we'll shop for our ring tomorrow because our big day is soon."

The next day we looked in the phone book for all the jewelry stores to save time.

After we purchased our rings, we stopped to eat at a nice restaurant. The rings were beautiful. We were excited about our big day.

After dinner, we took a stroll through the mall, then we bought some chocolates from the See's Candies store. Of course, we ate a few on the way home! Yum that's what we ate for our dessert. We bought a pound of caramel squares with walnuts covered with dark chocolate. We bought peanut clusters too. They tasted so good. Finally, we made it back at home. We had our showers and relaxed.

We listened to some music, the song was by the Five Satins, "In the Still of the Night."

I didn't go to sleep right away. I was too excited about our wedding day. I got out of bed to try my wedding gown on one more time. After I put it on, I put on my white patent leather high heel shoes. I got a good look at myself in the bathroom mirror getting practice walking in my heels.

I didn't realize how long I'd been in the bathroom. When Harold woke up, he called me with urgency. He didn't see me in the bed next to him. It startled him. He called out loud for me. I yelled back to him. I'll be there in a minute. This time when I got in the bed he wrapped his arms around me tight. It wasn't long before we both fell asleep. It was Thursday morning the day before our wedding. With a smile, he wrapped his arms around me and said, "Babe, tomorrow morning we'll be on our way to Tijuana."

We got up early, it was Friday morning. We decided to have breakfast after we got to San Diego. We didn't dress for our wedding until we got to Tijuana. We packed our wedding apparel in garment bags.

After being on the highway for 2 ½ hours, we stopped in San Diego to have our breakfast, lunch, and dinner. We also spent the night in a motel. We had a good night sleep. Early Saturday morning we put on our wedding clothes before leaving San Diego. We didn't have much further to drive to be in Tijuana. When we got there, he hugged me and said, "Baby, you're my beautiful angel. This is our big day." I styled the back of my hair into a French roll. The front part of my hair had curls combed to one side of my face. It was covering one eye. I wore my oval-shaped rhinestone silver pierced earrings.

As we were driving, he began to sing a little bit of the song "Going to the Chapel," the song by The Dixie Cups. I looked at him in amazement and said to him, I didn't know you could sing. "Baby we have a life time to explore each other because this is just the beginning." (Now that I've written my story at age 74, I think about the things he told me at age14. I was too young to know how to be a wife.)

When we got to the chapel, the sign in the window said, "CLOSED. We'll return in 15 minutes." We parked right in front waiting for the Clergy to return. We saw a hand reach into the window and remove the sign. With a big smile on his face when he got out of the car to come open my door. He extended his hand to help me out. We hurried into the Wedding Chapel. We glanced at ourselves in the mirror as we entered the chapel making sure my veil looked good over my face. The preacher offered us a seat while he called his wife to come play the organ.

Chapter 8c - Parent's Consent For Marriage

The preacher's wife asked me to lift my veil so she could see my beautiful face. After I lifted my veil she said, you look mighty young. She asked, "Young man how old is your fiancé?" Harold looked at me and said, "Baby you tell him your age." The preacher and his wife said, "We need a written consent from your parents before you can get married."

When we left Tijuana, he sped on the freeway so fast, it didn't take us long to get home.

We arrived in Venice around 4:00 that evening. We sat in the car for a moment; Harold told me to tell my parent's that I was pregnant. The truth was I wasn't pregnant. But he said, my parents would give me their consent to get married if I said that I was pregnant. We knocked at the front door. My father answered with a surprised look on his face. Harold greeted my father with a hand shake. He expressed his love for me. He let my parents know we wanted to get married. He said, "Mr. and Mrs. Beckham, I tried to marry your daughter, but we need your consent because of her age.

My father invited us into the house. My mother was sitting nearby in the living room. Harold and I stood as he shook her hand and introduced himself. He explained that we needed a written consent from them. My mother said, "Yes I heard what you said." In a hurry, she reached for her writing tablet and pen that was on the lamp table. She wrote so fast it would make your head spin. After receiving the written consent, I gave my parents a hug and thanked them. We didn't stay long because we were tired from the long trip and headed to our apartment.

On our way home, he said, "Baby we'll have to wait until next week to go back to Tijuana, I need to work all week." He cared about me. When he told my parent's that he was going to take good care of me; that really melted my heart.

When we got home he picked me up and carried me into the apartment. He said, "Baby I'm giving you a nice warm lotion massage." Okay Honey, that'll feel good. He heated a pot of water to warm the bottle of lotion. He was wearing his briefs while rubbing the warm lotion on my body. "Baby, lay on your back, this time." He began messaging my neck taking his time all the way down to my feet. All I could say was, "Aw- woo- umm- honey!"

Chapter 8d - Getting Married

We got a good night sleep. We got up at 9:00 Sunday morning. We showered and had a late breakfast. He cooked because I didn't know how. We had Jimmy Dean sausage, hashed brown potatoes, scrambled eggs, and golden-brown toast with strawberry jam and a hot cup of coffee. I watched him while he prepared breakfast because I wanted to learn how to cook. It was my first time eating pork meat. It was so delicious.

Later that day we went to the movie. We didn't have far to go to the Fox Theater. It was a 10-minute drive from our home. We saw Elvis Presley's first movie when it first came out.

While we were waiting to go back to Tijuana, after he got off work he'd teach me how to play dominos.

Finally, it was the Friday. We were so happy to go back to Tijuana. We had my parent's written consent this time. If we would have given a thought, Harold could've written a consent for me to marry. I don't think the preacher and his wife would've known the difference. (Duh!) When we arrived in Tijuana this time we knew exactly where to find the Wedding Chapel. When we got there, it was open. Only this time we waited until we got to the chapel to get dressed for our wedding. Harold paid for the wedding fee the last time we were there. It didn't take the preacher long to marry us.

Our wedding only lasted fifteen minutes. We went to shop at a few stores there in Tijuana and drove to San Diego. We spent the night there before going home. My husband promised he'd buy me more clothes as soon as he saved some extra money.

He said," Baby if you learn how to cook we can save money. Then I can buy you more clothes." I tried to cook a few dishes from a recipe book he bought for me. I still didn't cook the food right. I asked my husband "Is it okay if my sister could come over to teach me how to cook?" He thought it was a good idea and agreed. That way we could save some money. I was 14 and he was 6 ½ years older than me. He was a sharp dresser! He wanted me to dress sharp too! He wore leisure suits, Levi's and khaki pants with creases in them.

When I first got married at 14, I asked my sister to cook for us because I didn't know how to cook. One day my husband said to her, "Sis, your food is delicious." I got jealous of my sister because my husband complimented her for cooking. I wanted him to say my food tasted good too. I'd watch my sister cook. I ask her questions so I'd know when the food was fully cooked.

I learned how to cook in a week. I was so glad he liked my cooking too. The first thing I cooked was spaghetti and meatballs with pasta sauce. We had green beans sautéed in a buttery garlic sauce. We had garden salad with Italian dressing with French garlic toast. These are some of my favorite foods. We also had strawberry short cake with vanilla ice cream for dessert. Yum, yum! It's making me hungry right now.

I cooked every day that week. When we woke up on Saturday morning, he said, "Baby since you learned how to cook I'm taking you shopping." So let's go buy you some clothes. Wow! I was so excited. I gave him a great big hug and a kiss. He said, "I'm proud of you for learning how to cook, thanks babe." We ate a light breakfast before going shopping.

We went to the Santa Monica Mall. We saw coats on sale. I checked it out. Wow! I found a beautiful leopard print coat, I really liked it. It had a large collar with large decorative black buttons on top of the large collar buttoned to one side. It had a full flair style; it was very feminine and classy. I tried it on and fell in love with it. In addition to getting a coat, I got some black patent leather high heel shoes, a black evening dress with spaghetti straps with a built-in bra. It had a form fitting bodice. It was short length, a little above my knees.

I learned how to cook and every week he'd buy me more clothing to build up my wardrobe.

As we walked to the car, he said, "Baby just keep cooking those delicious meals, and I'll buy you more clothes." I was a happy teenager, but I felt like a woman in my new wardrobe and high heels. He said, "Baby now that you're a young lady, you need to learn how to drive.

Chapter 9

RAPED BY A STRANGER

It was a cloudy day in March of 1955, on a Saturday morning. My husband decided to give me a driving lesson. He drove the car as he instructed me how to drive. He parked near the curb, turned the ignition off, and then we switched seats. He instructed me as I adjusted the seat; to put one foot on the breaks and the other foot on the clutch to shift into drive. Then I drove down the residential streets. "Baby, hold your arm out the window in a horizontal position and turn right at the corner." As I made a wide right turn, I slammed into the man's car with the sound of a big bang.

He said, "Baby go home, I'll take the blame. While walking home a stranger was following me. He said, "Young lady wait. I saw you hit that car. If you go home the police will find you." If you come with me you'll be safe." At age 14, I didn't know what to do. I went to his apartment. He introduced himself as Virgil. After the stranger explained I'd be safe, I trusted him.

After we were inside his apartment, I had no idea what he was going to do. Immediately, he locked the door. He penned my arms behind me and pulled my panties off and raped me. I screamed. "I won't hurt you," He held his hand over my mouth to muffle the noise from my crying. I didn't know not to trust him. My husband was still at the scene of the accident to take the blame for me.

After he raped me I felt filthy. It was awful. After I left, I was afraid my husband might be home. To my surprise he wasn't there. I rushed into the bathroom, took a warm bath, put on perfume, and cleaned clothes. When my husband came home I was sitting on the sofa crying. When he put his arms around me I evaded him. He said, "Baby why are you crying? I already took the blame for the accident. So just relax and don't worry. I never told my husband that Virgil raped me; because I was afraid he might hurt me.

I was so angry that he took advantage of me. I wished I would've kicked Virgil in his private parts when he raped me. Then he'd have something to think about. I was terrified when I wrecked my husband's car and it made things worse after Virgil raped me.

Chapter 9a - Nicknamed Sittin Bull

After a few days, my husband and I were getting back to normal after I wrecked our car. After we ate dinner he said, "Honey I'm going to my friend's house to play some cards." Okay. I responded. It was seven o'clock in the evening when he left. I wasn't worried about the time, until it started getting dark. When I noticed the time, it was 9:45 and I thought he should be coming home. It kept getting later and later. I was afraid of being alone, but he didn't leave a telephone number for me to call him.

Every time I heard a car drive up in front of our apartment, I thought it was him. I was getting upset! Several cars drove up to the apartment, but it still wasn't his car! At 2:30 a.m., I heard a car stop in front of our apartment. Then I heard the footsteps stop at my apartment door. I got out of bed. Then I tipped toed quietly to the front door. I stood there in the dark room!

I heard keys rattling in the keyhole at the front door. He opened it slowly. He reached his hand inside feeling for the light switch on the wall. I was in the dark with my fist balled up. As soon as he leaned his head inside of the door, I hit him in the eye! I gave him two quick punches in the eye as hard as I could. Wham! Bam! In pain, he grabbed his eye. He grunted as he said Ah! Ah! While he was falling onto the reclining chair. He kept moaning while still holding his eye. The chair was sitting next to the front door. After he finished groaning and moaning he said to me, "Kamiah why did you do that?" (LOL)

Before answering him, I wrapped some ice in a washcloth. I held it on his eye.! At the same time, I gave him sympathy but I wasn't sorry. I just didn't want him to retaliate. I said to him, "Honey I was scared and upset because you stayed away too long. I'm sorry." I was so glad he didn't hit me back. He accepted my apology.! We made up. I really didn't know I had such a temper until that night he stayed out gambling too long.

After I punched him in the eye he never left me alone after dark again. Instead, he began taking me with him to the gamble. (LOL)

Years later, after I punched my husband in his eye, he told our daughter that he nick-named me "Sitting Bull." She was 30, then. (LOL) Now when my grown children see me upset they call me Sittin Bull.

On day, my husband was teaching me how to drive his car. It was his new 1955 Chevy Coupe. While I was driving, he told me to make a right turn. There was a car at the stop sign, when I turned the corner, I wreck into the car that was there. My husband told me to go home, so, he could take the blame for me. I left the scene of the accident. I was on my way home. A man was following me. He said, wait little girl. If you go home the police will find there. There are people who saw you when you wrecked the man's car. Come to my house. Then police won't find you there.

I trusted the man. Plus, I didn't want the policeman to arrest me. So I went to the man's apartment. After we were inside his place, he locked the door. He grabbed both my arms. Then he pushed me down on a mattress lying on the floor. He ripped my panties off and raped me.

When Harold and I married, I was a virgin. We couldn't have sex until my period was over. But we had sex a week after our wedding day. I was afraid to tell my husband about the man that raped me. I thought he'd be angry with me. When I found out that I was pregnant, I was hoping the baby belonged to my husbands.

I was five months pregnant and my stomach was larger. He bought me a maternity outfit to wear. Whatever I wanted he would get it. One day I was craving Hershey chocolate with almonds; he would buy me 5 candy bars a day.

One evening, he surprised me with a case of Hershey candy bars. By looking at so much candy, I got sick eating it. My cravings changed. Next, I was craving Banana Split with vanilla ice cream with hot chocolate and nuts on top. He couldn't figure out a way to stock up on Banana Splits.

But he came up with another solution. He bought all the ingredients for a Banana Split for me to make it at home.

Chapter 9b - Husband Goes To Jail

It was a hot summer evening, in August 1955. I was sitting living room on the sofa. I had my arms stretched out on the back of the sofa. The ceiling fan was blowing cool air on my face. I was 5 months pregnant. I had been married for six months to my husband. I was craving a Banana Split. So my husband said, "Come on Babe, let's go get a Banana Split at Foster Freeze. It was 7:30 in the evening. When we drove away from the Foster Freeze Ice Cream Stand, he made a quick U-turn in the middle of the street. He slammed his foot on the breaks to stop!

He jumped out of the car in a hurry. I had no idea what he was up to. He didn't say a word to me. He left the car door open with the motor running. He ran toward the woman walking on the sidewalk. In a split second, he snatched her purse. The woman screamed! "Help! Somebody call the police." The police were there before he could get away. In a few minutes, four police cars were there. They arrested him. Three officers grabbed and handcuffed him. The fourth officer was a female. She came to the passenger's side of the car to talk to me.

I was frightened. The female officer asked me, "Did you know he was going to rob that woman?" No Officer, I didn't know what he was up to.

I cried as I said, I didn't do anything. "I'm sorry but we'll have to take you to juvenile hall to check your background." She asked, "What is your full name and age?" I cried so hard. My name is

Kamiah Nancy Gibbon, I'm 15, and I'm 5 months pregnant.

I called my mother after being in juvenile Hall for a few hours. I asked if I could stay with her and dad. I had nowhere to live. She asked, "Why aren't you with your husband?" Mother, he's in jail. What did he do?" He robbed a woman at gun point and took her purse. After I explained I wasn't involved in the robbery, then mother came to get me.

"How long will he be in jail?" I don't know, until he gets a trial date. My mother said, "If I have any trouble out of you, you're going to live somewhere else. Do you understand that?" Yes, I understand. My mother told me about her rules that I had to follow. She said, "I need you to help out with the chores, and to be home before the sun goes down. Another thing "When you're not going somewhere to take care of business I want you home. Is that understood?" Yes Mother, I will. I was on good behavior while staying with my parents. I didn't want to go back to the girl's school.

My mother took me grocery shopping with her and treated me to an ice cream cone. It was a scoop of vanilla and chocolate. Yummy! it was good. We sat in the car to enjoy it while we talked. I really liked the quality time we spent together. It was a few minutes but I enjoyed it. She never had the time to do it in the past. This was the first time we ever sat down to talk one on one. My mother asked, "How do you like being married now?" It's okay. I just hope he doesn't get into more trouble when he gets out of jail." So she said, "Yes, I hope he learned his lesson."

When I was at my parent's home for a week, I received a subpoena for me to go to my husband's trial. The judge asked, "What's your relationship to the defendant?" I'm his wife. The judge requested, "What were you doing when your husband snatched the woman's purse?" Your honor, I was sitting in the car.

"Kamiah did he discuss his intent with you regarding the robbery?" No, your honor, he just told me we were going to go get ice cream and that's all I knew.

The judge asked, "Mr. Gibbon did you snatch the lady's purse?" Yes, your honor, "Why did you rob this young lady?" Your Honor, my wife is 5 months pregnant and she wants things I can't afford." "What about getting a job Mr. Gibbon?" "Your Honor, I've been looking but no one is hiring right now." The Judge said, "Being out of work is no excuse to rob another person of their possession." The Judge declared him guilty of the crime and sentenced him to 7 months in the L.A. County Jail.

If I would have known Harold would rob people before we married, I never would've been his wife. My parents were shocked that he had committed a crime. They said, "He promised to take care of you." When he went to jail I didn't know where I was going to live.

Being so young I had no idea of how to take care of myself. He didn't want children and expected me to get an abortion. I wanted my baby, and I wasn't going to get an abortion. My mother taught me to have an abortion was a sin. I understand now that God has a purpose and a plan for everyone, and we don't have the right to take a life. I'm so glad I kept my baby.

I was asleep on the sofa bed at my parents' home. It was the morning of December 19, 1955. I awakened suddenly with labor pains. I cried, "Mother my stomach hurts." She said, "It's time for the baby to be born. Let's go to the hospital." I stayed in my night gown, and I put my coat over it. It was cold that time a year. It took us 40 minutes to drive from Venice to East Los Angeles; to the County General Hospital.

After several hours of labor the baby wasn't ready to be born yet. After walking more than six hour my labor pains were getting closer together. It was 12:00 noon, I could feel the pressure of my baby's head bearing down on my pelvis. I thought it was because I had to use the restroom. After I sat on the toilet, I felt my baby's head coming out. I yelled for help. A lady heard me moaning and crying. She asked, "Young lady what's wrong?"

"It's time to give birth. I feel my baby's head trying to come out. So the woman rushed out of the restroom to find a nurse. The nurse returned in a hurry because the baby's head was coming out. The nurse hurried back with a wheelchair and pushed me into the delivery room. I cried with pain. My hands gripped the armrest on the wheel chair so tight my hands were sore for a week. When I got to the delivery room the anesthesia doctor asked the nurse to pass him the ether to sedate me.

I started singing the Platter's song, "Oh yes, I'm the great pretender." Next, I heard a sound like a train running down the track. It felt like the train was rolling across my stomach. When the nurse woke me up she said, "Mrs. Gibbon you gave birth to a 4lb 5oz bouncing boy. He was laying in the bassinette sleeping next to my bed. She lifted him out and laid him in my arms. He was asleep, and I admired him as I was thinking of a name for him.

After looking at my baby boy for a while, I kept saying names out loud until the right name matched him. These are the names I chose from: Mitchell, Matthew, and Michael. The moment I said Michael that was it. That name really matched him. Then I thought about my oldest sister's son's name Leland, that's how I came up with his middle name.

Michael Leland sounded good to me and that was what I named him. I was only 15.6 years old. A lady came into the restroom just at the right time to call the nurse, because my baby was about to fall in the toilet.

Chapter 9c - An Angel Saved My Baby's Life

I was happy to be a mother. My husband was in jail for six months and we had nowhere to live. My baby and I lived with my parents until my husband returned. We moved into his cousin's apartment. His cousin was blind, but he got around very well.

After we lived with his cousin for two weeks, we had gone to bed and I fell fast asleep. That night the street lights shone through the sheer curtains at the windows; just enough to see without turning on a light in the apartment. We were sleeping on the sofa in the living room.

When he got out of bed it woke me up. I lay there quietly watching him lean over the baby's bassinette placing the pillow inside. I had my eyes barely opened pretending to be asleep watching his every move. He looked at me to make sure I was asleep while he was moving toward the baby's bassinette. I pretended to be asleep. It was just enough moonlight shining in the room so I could see him with my eyelids barely closed. I believe my angel woke me up just in time. I saw him getting closer to the bassinette. It was about two feet away from our sofa bed. I kept as still as I could while watching to see what he was going to do next.

So when I saw him lift the pillow up and put it in the bassinette I asked, "Harold what's wrong with the baby?" He said, "Oh no I'm just covering him up." He didn't know I was awake when he first picked up the pillow. I didn't say anything to him I just watched. The moon light was shining through the sheer curtains. I know he was getting ready to put a pillow over my baby's face because he looked suspicious.

I heard on the news about babies who died from crib deaths. I felt in my spirit or may I say I had a strong intuition that he was about to smother my baby boy. My husband never said that Michael was not his son, but I do believe that he knew that it wasn't his child.

My son's complexion was the same as the man who raped me. Unfortunately, I didn't know I was pregnant by him. I could see that my son didn't resemble my husband. But it still didn't dawn on me that Virgil was the father. I knew that Harold wasn't telling me the truth when he said he was just covering up the baby that night. I thank God that he didn't get a chance to kill my baby.

After giving birth, I was naïve about how I got pregnant from the man who raped me. All I knew is I missed my monthly period and my stomach was getting larger. I had a very small waistline before then. When I couldn't fit into my regular clothes I knew something had changed. I was pregnant.

My son was three months old when we moved in with his cousin. My husband and I expected to live with his cousin for two months. But after his cousin made sexual advance toward me, my husband moved us out of there in a hurry.

So I took a little sip of mint gin and it tasted okay. So Julie teased me again and said, "Girl you can't drink." "Turn the bottle up and drink it." She thought it was funny. It was about a fourth of a cup of mint gin left in the bottle. So I showed her that I could turn the bottle up and drink it all until it was gone. It wasn't long before I felt like the whole room was spinning around and I couldn't walk straight and everyone was laughing at me. I was only 15, I never had liquor before that day.

She didn't know I'd been drinking. She gave him to me to hold because he was crying. He was 3 months old. I held my son while I was standing and tried to cover him with his receiving blanket. When I placed him on my shoulder, he flipped off my shoulder from the standing position, and he landed on the floor head first. It was a very serious fall. Then Julie told our mother-in-law that I'd been drinking Mint Gin.

I bent over to pick up my screaming baby. In a hurry, my mother-in-law pushed me aside so she could pick him up. I was so drunk that I got nauseated. I ran to the bathroom to vomit, and that was the last thing I remembered. I didn't wake up until the next day. It was Sunday afternoon when I woke up in my bed. I asked my husband, "How did I get in bed?" So he said, "I picked you up off the bathroom floor and put you to bed." "So how do you feel now?" He replied. "I have a headache and I'll never drink anything that looks green, I hate mint gin." His brother Jeffrey and our sister-in-law had left Saturday evening.

It was Sunday afternoon when they came back. I was sitting in the living room feeding my baby. My husband went to the market to buy extra groceries while we lived with his mother. The doorbell rang. I answered the front door. It was Julie, my sister-in-law. I let her trick me into getting drunk the day before. But when she came back the next day, she laughed and made fun of me. She said, "Do you want to drink some more mint gin?" I said, "No! I'll never drink any green drinks again. I don't care what it is."

My husband and I were married a little over a year. My son Michael was three months old when I realized that I was three months pregnant with my second child. My husband didn't like it because I was pregnant again. So, he told me get an abortion. He bought some quinine and castor oil and told me to take it. When he gave it to me, I went to the bathroom and I pretended to take it. But I flushed it down the toilet.

I said to myself, forget him. I'm keeping my baby. I thank God, I kept her. I know that I did the right thing. (She is 60 years old now! She is a minister of the gospel.) We lived with his parent's until I was 6 months pregnant. Then one day my husband told me that his mother said we needed to move. I was tired of moving so much, but I didn't realize I was part of the problem of having to move. Every time I broke up with Harold he would vacate the apartment. After reconciling with him, we had to find a new place to live. He asked a couple who were his friends if they could share their small apartment with us and we'd split the rent.

Chapter 10

PREGNANT AND PARALYZED

One evening, he brought a case of watermelons home to me. He made sure I had enough of them to eat. He had them delivered by truck. Anderson helped him lift the gigantic box from the truck. They left it on the front porch. It was huge. It was about 50 watermelons in that huge box. He called me outside to see it. I was amazed. Oh, my goodness, I said. My eyes got big. I said, "why did you get so many?" He said, "Now you won't have to wait until I get home to have watermelons." I shared the melons with the couple. They didn't have a taste for watermelons like I did. Doll said, "Kamiah your baby is going to come here looking like a watermelon. We had a good laugh.

The couple decided to move out of the apartment and let us have it. We took possession of renting the place. I assumed Harold had paid the rent for the current month. Instead, he decided to abandon my son and me. The landlord knocked on the door to ask for the rent. "My husband has gone over for a month, I don't know where he is?"

Two weeks after he left me, I went outside picking up trash off the front lawn. The weeds had grown tall and the lawn needed mowing. I walked across the yard barefoot. Accidently, I stepped on a rusty nail. It was in a board hidden in the grass. The nail went deep into my foot. My foot was bloody with a lot of pain. I yelled! Somebody to help me. But nobody came to help me. After injuring my right foot, I had to hop on the left foot to the front porch to sit down. I wrapped my foot with some paper napkins to stop the blood.

I was sitting on the front porch. My leg was leaning on the bush nearby. I felt something bit my left leg. It was itching, so, I scratched it. I had to hop on my left leg to get to the inside of my apartment. My right foot was injured by the rusty nail. So in order to go inside my apartment, I had to hop on my left. I lifted my seven-month-old son out of his play pen to hold and feed him. After feeding him, I laid him down next to me. After a few minutes, I discovered I couldn't get off the sofa. My legs felt numb and I couldn't move them. I was desperate and terrified. I sat there and cried so hard until my baby started crying too.

We cried together for quite some time. I didn't know what to do. (I didn't have a telephone to dial 911) The only thing I could think of to do was to call on God. I cried, "Oh God, please help me. After I cried out to God, I didn't feel afraid anymore. I stopped crying. I had to face the fact; that I was pregnant and paralyzed. I had to take care of myself. I had no other choice. My baby cried so long, he cried himself to asleep. I lay down on my side and slid my body off the sofa to get down on the floor. I used my hands and elbows to pull myself across the floor to get around in the house.

It was July 1956, my mother-in-law, Marie Crown, happened to come by to visit me. Oh my God! As I write my story today, that was no mistake that she came by that day. I said, "Lord thank you for watching over me. After she saw my condition, she asked, "Kim what's wrong with you?" I cried, "I don't know." She asked, "Why don't you let me keep your baby until you get better?" I agreed with her. I thought it was a good idea. As a result, she picked my son up from the sofa, washed him up, and put clean clothes on him. She gathered up the rest of his clothes and left with him. I let her take my son because I believed she'd give him back to me. She promised when I was better she'd give him back.

As I reflect over my life, I know God watched over me. A few moments after my mother-in-law left with my son, I heard a knock at the door. I crawled on my elbows to open the door. I was shocked. It was my cousin Butch. I hadn't seen him in 10 years. He was 8 and I was 6 the last time we lived in Las Vegas, Nevada, at the same time. (Now we're in our teens, I was 16 and he was 18.) Wow! For such a time as this. (As I write this story, I realize it was no accident for my cousin to show up just at the right time.) Now I know God sent my cousin to help me. (I praise God.)

He drove me to my parent's home. I waited in the car, so he could go and get my mother. He told my mother what had happened to me. "Nancy is paralyzed from the waist to her feet. She needs to go to the emergency room." He said, "Aunt Elsie, I'm glad I went by to visit her." My mother came to the car and asked, "Where is your husband?"

I have no idea. He left me a month ago! I replied. I was crying! My mother said, "Wait until I lock the door." She hurried back to the car; then we were on our way to the hospital."

As soon as we reached the emergency room, the nurse checked my vital signs.

He gave me another shot to prevent lockjaw from the rusty nail I stepped on. The doctor said that if I had waited a few hours longer I could've died. The doctor told me that it was a miracle that my unborn baby survived too. I didn't know it at first, but the doctor said I was bit by a black widow spider. When I left the hospital, my mother took me to her home until she found a place for me to live.

Chapter 11

FOUND A GOOD MAN

August 1956, my parents didn't have enough room for me to live with them. She took me to live with my cousin Ruth. I was 8 months pregnant with my second child. I'd been living with her for about a week when I heard a knock at the door. It was her friend named Erwin. He said, "Open the door. I brought you some wine. Open up." She drank wine every day and Erwin was her drinking partner.

When she opened the door, I heard a voice that sounded like my husband. He came in with Erwin. I thought, this sure is a small world. How did my husband know I was here? He really didn't know I was there. He was just hanging out with my brother-in-law. I really think it was a coincidence. Later I found out my husband and Erwin who is my brother-in-law just happened to be out together because they were friends. I found out that day that they were friends of my cousin Ruth.

As soon as I heard my husband's voice, I ran into the kitchen. I was curious why my husband was at my cousin's house. When I peeked around the corner of the kitchen doorway, we saw each other at the same time! He was surprised to see me. His oriental shaped eyes got big. He bugged his eyes and stood up as he rushed to grab me. I ran into the bedroom. I tried to shut the door but he grabbed me before I could get away. He picked me up and squeezed my knees and my back together so hard. I was 8 months pregnant. He squeezed my stomach extremely hard while he carried me outdoors.

I screamed for help. I felt severe pain in my stomach. I believe he tried to make me have a miscarriage. I yelled, "Somebody helped me." My stomach was hurting. Someone called the police. It didn't take long for them to get there. My husband was still holding me in his arms while I was screaming. Upon the officer's arrival, he asked us our names. The Officer asked, "What is the problem between you two?" "Officer, I was trying to get my wife to come home where she belongs."

"Mr. Gibbon, did you ever hit your wife?" The Officer asked. "No Sir," my husband replied. "Mrs. Gibbon, did your husband the truth? Yes, Officer. But when I was 7 months pregnant and paralyzed, my husband left me to die. I thank God that my cousin found me just in time to take me to the hospital. This is the first day my husband came back to get me."

My husband tried to make me have a miscarriage when I was eight months pregnant. He squeezed my stomach between my back and knees, real hard. "Do you want to press charges against him?" "Yes, officer I do." The two officers arrested him. I went back into my cousin's house.

The next day following my husband's arrest, a man knocked on the front door. He came to ask, if I was okay. He said he heard me screaming when my husband tried to take me against my will. Lee was my cousin's neighbor. She was so sloppy drunk, she could hardly stand up. She slurred her words as she introduced us. "Lee, this is my cousin Kamiah." After she introduced us, she flopped down real hard on the sofa. I spread a blanket over her because she was in nothing but her underwear. Lee said, "Young lady how are you doing today?" I'm doing fine thank you. "I saw you yesterday when that man was holding you. You were screaming for help. I wanted to know if you were alright."

"I was the one who called the police, because it looked like you were having a problem with him." "May I ask who was he?" He is my husband. Then Lee said, "I really don't like getting into your business, but it looked like he was hurting you. May I ask did he hurt you?" "Yes, he did." Lee asked, "Do you need to go to the doctor?" "No, I'll be alright." "Why did he try to hurt you?" he asked.

"He left me to die a month ago, I began crying as I said, my mother brought me over here to stay with my cousin. I didn't have anywhere else to live. Lee said, "I live across the street in the back house. Your husband won't find you over there. If he did find you I wouldn't let him harm you. I have friends that work for the police department. All I must do is call them they would be here before you could blink your eyes!

How would you like to come and stay with me? He said to me, you deserve to be cared for, not mistreated. I'll take care of you. I'll cook for you also. All you need to do is take care of yourself and your baby. I thought about my situation and how Lee came to rescue me, I figured I had nothing to lose. So I said "Okay, I'll stay with you."

My cousin was sleeping; I woke her up so she could lock the door. I was leaving. Lee asked to take me to dinner with him. I was glad he asked, because I was hungry. He said, "There's a Mexican restaurant a few blocks down the street. Do you like Mexican food?" Yes, I sure do. He got his car out the garage so we could drive to the restaurant. I was eight months pregnant, but I looked like I was four months instead.

He asked, "When is the baby due?" The baby is due next month! He said, "You don't look large enough to be eight months." He smiled as he said, "Only you should know how many months you are."

Lee was a nice man. He treated me so kind. He never asked me for any favors for his kindness. He knew how to do just the right things at the right time. After that we went back to his apartment. He said "Kim "I'd like to get to know you better. I'd like for you to stay with me if you want to. (There were so many things going through my mind. I wondered why he wants to do all this for me. We barely knew one another. I just met him.) He continued to tell me what he thought of me. He said, "You deserve to be treated like a woman. I will make sure you and the baby are treated good. I am going to buy a home next year. I have a good job.

As we sat on the sofa watching television he said, "I want you to think it over. Tell me how you feel about the idea?" "I'll think about it." Lee was so nice to me. Every day he made sure I had everything in the house I needed before he went to work. He'd call me on his lunch break. He wanted to make sure I was okay.

He slept on the sofa while I slept in his bed. He never tried to have sexual intercourse with me. It made me happy that he had respect for me. I asked "Lee, are you a Christian?" He said, "I sure am." He asked if I had received Christ into my heart as Lord and Savior. Yes, I'm a Christian too. I asked, "How old are you?" "I am 25. Is that too old for you?" I really liked how well he was treating me and I answered him, "Oh no, you're not too old. I was 16 at that time.

Whenever I felt discomfort from being pregnant, he would massage my back and legs. He said, "I care about you because you are a young woman expecting a child and need someone to take care of you. My heart was melting with his kindness every day. By the time the weekend came I had time to think it over. So I let him know, I'd to like to stay with him.

It was the first week in December of 1956 that was a Saturday morning. He was off to work, so he cooked breakfast for us. He asked, "Would you like to go to a movie this afternoon?" "It sounds like a good idea," "Yes I'd love to go to the movie." After lunch, we went to a movie. Then we went window shopping at the mall he bought me a nice robe, nightgown, and slippers. He said, "I want you to have something nice to wear after the baby is born. "Is that alright with you?" I thought "Wow! He is so nice to me." "Yes, I'd love to have them. But I don't know how I'm going to pay you back. I had been living with him for 3 weeks. One day while he was at work, I was craving a taco dinner. So I walked four blocks from his apartment to a Mexican restaurant. While I was walking, I heard car wheels screeching in the middle of the street. It came to a sudden halt. I didn't recognize the car.

But when the person got out of the car, it was my husband. When I saw him, I was terrified. I didn't want my husband to be out of jail that soon. He hurried out of the car to grab me. I screamed. Somebody help me.

He said, "Kamiah I'm not going to hurt you. I'm taking you home where you belong. I don't want you out on the streets. Come on get in the car. I promise I won't hurt you." So I went home with him. I thought about all the clothes Lee had bought for the baby and me. I was sorry I had to leave him. I was afraid to tell Harold that I was living with him. I felt bad having to leave after I found a good man, because a good man is hard to find.

Chapter 12

AFTER BIRTH ILLNESS

After I got into the car with him, my husband drove around town until he found a telephone booth. We stopped at a gasoline service station to call his Aunt Ella. He asked if we could stay with her until our baby was born. Thank God, she said "Yes." I was tired of moving from house to house. I was nine months pregnant. I made up my mind to trust my husband to take care of me again. It was a good feeling to have him going to work every day and came home every evening. A week after we were living with his Aunt and Uncle, he took me out to dinner. When we came back we went to our room to watch television before we went to bed.

That night at 10:00 we settled in bed to go to sleep. Since we were tired. It didn't take us long to fall asleep. I woke up early that morning at 6:00 feeling energetic. I helped Aunt Ella do some chores around the house. She said, "Daughter, your baby is going to be born soon. How do you know that, Auntie? Well, you're getting restless is one of the signs before a child is born."

It took us 25 minutes to drive from Venice to Westwood, California to the U.C. L. A. Hospital. We were almost there when my water broke. We arrived there just in the nick of time. My husband stopped the car right in front of the emergency room entrance. A nurse was close by and requested a wheel chair. The nurse came to help and asked, "Is this your first baby?" I said "No, this is my 2nd. "She rushed me into the labor room and prepared me for delivery. I suddenly moaned as I felt one big hard pain in my abdomen and then another hard pain came as I grunted. The nurse said to "Push hard Kamiah!" It was so painful, I said, "Oh God, help me"

The nurse said, "Take a deep breath slowly, inhale and exhale. The nurse cut a small incision to enlarge the vagina opening to help with the birth. She said, "The incision will feel like a little sting and it'll be done." I said to the nurse with a sigh of relief, "Wow! It's finally over." I heard my baby cry when she made her entrance into the world. But the nurse said, "No, the first part is over as she said; "Now I need to sew your incision back together." "It'll be a few stitches and then you can relax, okay?" I replied, "Okay."

After the birth of my baby girl I saw the nurse give her a bath. "Here's your beautiful baby girl. She lay her in my arms as she said, "You can hold her for a few minutes until your room is ready. My baby was born before the doctor arrived. They didn't have time to sedate me. She was born at 2:33 a.m. When the doctor finally got there, I had already given birth to my baby!

All the doctor did was look at my wrist band and pressed down on my stomach. He tapped me on the arm and said, "Kamiah you're doing fine. You'll be going home in five days, okay?" My husband came to visit me the first day our daughter was born. He bought me a beautiful pink night gown, slippers, and a robe to match. "Honey I'll bring the baby's clothes when you're ready to come home."

I celebrated New Year's Eve in the hospital. My sisters and a few friends came to visit on New Year's Day. They kept me laughing so the time went by faster. They told me to enjoy the service from the nurses while I had the chance. I was happy to be going home on the 4th of January 1957. My husband bought her a beautiful little pink and white gown with a matching blanket. We left the hospital to return to his uncle and aunt's house.

My husband and I lived with his Aunt and Uncle. My father and mother came to visit us. When my father saw our baby girl Patricia, he said "Good night. She is a beautiful work of art." When my father really liked something, he'd express his self by saying "Good night. Whenever he said,

"Good night" and stretched the word "Good" by stretching the "O's," then you knew he really liked something. He liked it from the bottom of his heart when he said it that way.

My father was a jolly dad. When something was funny to him he'd get a good deep-down belly laugh. My baby girl was just five days old and everyone who saw her said she looked like a Japanese doll. She had slanted eyes, a head full of black straight hair, rosy pink lips, and cheeks.

My father was so proud of his family tree and he'd let us know it! My mother never gave me a compliment. I guess she didn't know how to do that! But she sure knew how to let me know whenever I did something wrong. I suppose that is the way she grew up. She never made any compliments about my children. I thought my mother didn't like me because she never said anything good about me. One day it dawned on me that my mother couldn't give me compliments because she never got them from her parents But I understand it now that I'm an adult.

After living with my husband's relatives for one week, his aunt said that we needed to move. I'll never forget. It was a windy, cold, rainy night. When he came home from work, we packed and moved out of their house that night.

So he called a friend of his who was an elderly man. He asked him if we could stay with him until our baby was a little older. The man said that we could stay with him. Thank God! I said. So I put my clothes on, wrapped up in my coat, a scarf, and wrapped our baby in her blanket, so we would be warm. We tried to keep warm and dry but I got wet anyhow. A few days after we moved I became very ill.

After my baby was born I didn't know the nurse left the afterbirth in me! It caused me to be very ill! I was bed ridden for three months! I got my head and feet soaked in the rainy weather! I was so ill; I nearly died. I was ill for three months. I couldn't even take care of my baby. My sister Rhonda came every day to take care of me and my baby. I went back to the hospital. The doctor found out that the afterbirth was still in me. I started feeling better I thank God for having mercy on me by healing me. I thank God for my sister Rhonda also. My husband and I, and our baby lived with an elderly man until our baby girl was about 5 months old.

Chapter 13

LEFT TOWN WITH A STRANGER

It was a hot summer day in July 1958, it was a nice day for the beach. A few weeks after my 18th birthday we rented a house from his cousin on 21st and Pico. They sold their home, so we had to move. We moved to the Ritz Hotel near the beach. From the sixth floor, I see the ocean and the beautiful sunsets. We lived near the Pacific Ocean Theme Park. It was on Pacific Ocean Boulevard in Santa Monica, California. My husband worked as a hotel clerk there. I worked as a maid, I cleaned the rooms. On my off days, I'd draw pictures of famous people from magazines for a hobby. I taught my 2-year-old daughter how to color in a coloring book. She would entertain herself quietly for hours after she learned how to color. She was a good baby.

We lived in a hotel suite that looked like a small apartment. The sofa let out into a bed in the living room. The kitchen and bathroom were small but that was home for us. It was a beautiful day when I decided to take my daughter out for a walk on the beach. We had been in the room long enough.

I went to the front desk looking for my husband, but he was gone. The other hotel clerk said, "Your husband went to take his break. It was the first time my husband went on a break without telling me. It upset me. He used to call me to find out what I cooked for lunch. Sometimes he'd ask if I want him to pick up something for lunch

When I saw another clerk at the desk I knew something was wrong. I asked the clerk, "Where is my husband?" He said, "Oh he stepped out for a minute." I waited for 30 minutes and he still hadn't returned. When he did return, he was with a woman. They were talking and holding hands.

He didn't expect to see me. I was sitting in the lobby waiting for him. So, he tried to play the scene off by telling me she was a relative. I didn't believe him. But I let him think I was okay with him being with her. But I was so upset I made plans to leave him.

So the next day, I packed a few clothes. I told my husband that my daughter and I were going to the beach. He gave me $50, he said, have a good time. I was still upset with him for cheating on me. So I left him! I had no idea about where we were going.

After my daughter and I had left, I saw a crowd gathering near the beach front. It was exciting to see the movie stars! They were producing a movie! My daughter was two-year-old. I dressed her in a beautiful pink dress with ruffles on the hem. She wore white leather shoes with it. We were walking down the street where all the action was taking place. The director said, "Take one,; camera and action." The actors were acting out their parts.

As she hurried away she threw us a kiss and yelled, "It was nice to meet you Kamiah and little Patricia. I hope to see you again sometime." We waved goodbye to her. It was such a thrill to get to meet a movie star in person. I felt so honored that she took a liking to my baby. I don't recall the name of the movie she was starring in. As my daughter and I watched Lana Turner she started acting her part. It must have been about 45 minutes that had gone by. We watched all the stars as they acted their parts.

A guy in the crowd noticed me. He came over where we were stand-ing to introduce himself to me. "My name is Chico I just got off the ship from Jamaica." He showed me where the huge ship was, by pointing at it anchored in the ocean.

He spoke to me with a Jamaican accent and said, "Young lady may I ask, what is your name?" My name is Kamiah. "That's a beautiful name, Kamiah." "You have an accent where are you from?" I'm a native of California. After we chatted awhile, I felt comfortable getting to know him.

Since I was leaving my husband for cheating on me. I let Chico influence me into leaving Venice. So I moved to Los Angeles with him! "Kamiah I'm going to visit my relatives in Los Angeles. Would you like to go with me?" Chico asked.

I don't know why, but I didn't have any fear of this guy. I was just looking for a way of getting away from my husband. I didn't know anything about Chico. "Yes, I'd like to go." Today, now that I think about it, it was my guardian angels who watched over me back in those days. I took a risky chance of going away with a stranger.

I was so naive then. I think about the news that I often hear of when young ladies get into a vehicle with a stranger and end up dead. It is so terrifying to think it could've happened to me.

My parents never taught me about strangers that they might hurt me. I never knew they could harm me. I was naïve at age 18. I came from protective parents and I had never talked to a stranger. I only knew Chico for a few hours. I ended up leaving town with him. He took me to Los Angeles the day I left my husband. I ended up being sorry for leaving my husband. When Chico took me to his bachelor apartment he said, "I told you I was going to visit my relatives. But I wanted to teach you how to make some money." I said "Chico, what are you talking about?" He said, "Well you and your baby have to eat, right?" I replied "Yes!" So, he said, "I'm going to teach you how to make some easy money." "How is that?" "Well, you know about sex because you have a baby." Am I right? Yes, I said.

Chico took me to 76th street and Central Avenue in Los Angeles where a lot of men worked. You can dress up and parade around on the sidewalk until a guy picks you up. He said, "Make sure you charge the guys $50.00 a trick." When he finished telling me how to be a prostitute, he left to take care of some business. Now that I think about it, for all I know he could've gone to bring someone back for my trick.

Since it was after six o'clock in the evening, the men were gone for the day. So, the next day he took me to start prostituting. He told me to wait at his apartment again until he came back. Instead of waiting, I left his apartment as soon as he was gone. I didn't like the idea of being a prostitute. I'm not going to be a prostitute, for nobody! I never heard of selling my body to men; it frightened me.

When he said I'd make a lot of money by sleeping with men, it made me sick to my stomach. Yuk! I thought, how awful. I thought running away with a stranger was the dumbest thing I ever did. I began to fear for my life. It's no telling what Chico might do to me and my daughter. I sensed it could be some serious trouble being there with him. I had to think quickly about what to do. I didn't know when he was coming back. I didn't know where in the world I was going. I was getting worried. I didn't know anything about Los Angeles neither the neighborhood he had brought us to.

My daughter and I fled in a hurry. We went to a Chinese Restaurant a few blocks away. There were a few other customers there. I was waiting for the waitress to bring our food. A man came in to order his food a few minutes after I ordered. I noticed he kept watching us. He came to our table and said, "Hello young lady, do you come here often?" No, it's my first time. I asked him, "Do you live around here?" "Yes, I live a few blocks down the street," he replied. He was about 5' 8" tall, well built with broad shoulders with a well-groomed haircut.

He wore a dark Kelly-green leisure suit. I noticed his high cheekbone with dimples on his cheeks. I saw his nice white even teeth as he smiled and introduced himself. "My name is Luther, and what is your name?" He asked. "My name is Kamiah and this is my daughter Patricia," I replied. He said, "You look like a movie star" I blushed as I smiled. "Kamiah is a pretty name," "You look like Kim Novak to me. I took a good look at him and said, "You resemble the actor Marlon Brando to me; do you mind if I call you Marlon?" "Yeah, it's okay, I like Marlon Brando!"

I was wearing a size 8 tiger print jump suit with a matching belt and had on my black high heel shoes. "Are you married?" He asked. "Yes, I am, but we are separated, and I've gotten myself into a situation I don't need to be in," I replied.

With a perplexed look on his face, Marlon asked, "What kind of situation did you get yourself into?" Tears rolled down my face, as I explained that I left my husband and ended up in a worse situation. I could barely talk because of my crying. Marlon told me not to cry; that everything will be alright. I stopped crying. I continued to explain. After I left my husband, I didn't have plans as to where I was going.

I made a serious mistake leaving home with a stranger. At the same time, I was talking to another stranger when I met Marlon. I knew I had to trust someone because Chico wanted to be my pimp and I was afraid. I cried and said to Marlon," I left home with a stranger." After telling him I left with a stranger, Marlon was trying to comfort me. When I cried my daughter began crying too. I had to stop crying so she would stop. She was 18 months old and didn't know why I was crying but it upset her. Marlon told me that he'd keep Chico from bothering me.

Chapter 14

1958 HOUSE PARTY FIGHT

"Kamiah realize your mistakes and don't do them again! Okay?" He said." Where are you going now?" As I answered him, I broke down and cried. "I don't know where to go." He said, "What do you want to do?" I began crying again. "I wish I'd stayed in Santa Monica because I don't know anyone in Los Angeles." My daughter started crying because she saw me crying.

Marlon put his hand on my shoulder and said, "Do you want me to drive you back to Santa Monica?" "No, I don't want to go because my husband and I might get into a fight." Marlon said, "I don't want to leave you and your baby out here." The customers were looking at us and talking among themselves. I suppose they wondered what was going on between Marlon and me because I constantly cried. He suggested that we at least go outside to talk privately. "Kamiah, you're welcome to come to my house. I have two sisters, a brother, and my brother-in-law who live with me." I'm sure they'll be glad to meet you. "What do you say about that?"

It was a nice warm summer night. The six of us crammed into his Lincoln Continental car going to the party. Once we drove to San Pedro, it didn't take us long to find the house Party. It was a beautiful two-story home in an influential neighborhood. The party room was huge with blue flashing lights. The chairs were sitting against the walls. So it would be room for dancing in the center of the room. The elegant lady of the house took us on a tour of their home. We got to the party earlier than the rest of the guest. Marlon's and I stood on the balcony; the gentle warm breeze blew across our faces. We admired ocean and the homes on the hillside.

Marlon asked, "Kim, how would you like to have a home like this?" "I sure would." "Kim, you'd have to make up your mind first if you're going to stay with Gibbon, I like you a lot." He wrapped his arms around me and held me tight. We stepped outside on the balcony to get fresh air from the warm summer breeze.

The house was in the hills of San Pedro, California. It had a breath-taking view. We could see the waves dashing up against the rock from the ocean. There was a ship sailing in the distance. There were people camping on the sandy beach front. The people who owned the house were co-workers and friends of Marlon's.

There were so many guests, it was hardly room enough to dance. When the doorbell rang, Mary called her husband John to answer the door because she was busy setting the food on the buffet table. John rushed downstairs to receive more guests. It was evident he didn't recognize the person because I heard the man say, "My name is Roy and this is my buddy Chico. When they came in they had to squeeze through the crowded floor while people were dancing. There were more guests arriving at 9:30 p.m.

Ben introduced his friend Arthur to John. John had invited Ben and his wife to the party. But, Ben didn't tell John that he and his wife had separated. So that's why Ben brought his friend with him.

Later on, that night John asked Ben, "Why didn't Sherri come with you?" Ben said to John, "Man, one day I came home and my baby was gone." In the meantime, John's wife Mary came into the family room to talk to Marlon and me. She slightly turned her head and raised her shoulder, as she rolled her eyes. She was making gestures with her hands, like rubbing her right hand slowly over her left hand up on her arm. She slowly moved her fingers over her wedding ring in a sensuous motion. That was her way of asking the question with body language. She had just asked us were we going to get married.

She moved her shoulders up and down slowly as she danced to the beat of the music. She kept dancing until she approached us. She said to Marlon, "I noticed you and Kim have been holding hands all evening. When is the big day?" As Marlon chuckled he said, "Mary you'll be one of the first to know." I laughed right along with him.

Mary asked, "What about it Kim?" I smiled and said, "Marlon will let you know our wedding date." Her husband was the DJ! He played the big 78 record albums. Some of the songs were "Hot Fun in the Summer Time," "Oh What a Night" by the Platters, "My Dearest Darling" by Etta James, and many more oldies but goodies. It was the music from the 1950s."

Marlon reached for my hand for me to stand up, for me to dance with him. After the dance was over, somebody grabbed our chairs.

Now I didn't have a place to sit. Rather than just stand there we continued to dance. We danced to every song. My feet were so sore. I was tired too. We stayed to ourselves in one corner. A guy saw us from across the room. He staggered across the room to where we were standing. He was so tipsy that he spilled his drink as he came toward us. He slurred his words as he said, "Man let me dance with your lady?"

I held on to Marlon, I whispered in his ear, "I don't want to dance with him, he's too drunk." He was the man that came in with Chico. He insisted on putting his hands on me. Marlon removed his hands off me. That's when the guy spilled his drink on me. He took a punch at Marlon trying to hit him in the eye. He missed hitting him, but hit the wall. I jumped out of the way. I found out later that his name was Roy. He was the one that came over to join Chico to fight Marlon.

When I first saw him, I didn't recognize Chico under the blue lights in the room. When I got a closer look at him I was shocked. I told Marlon, don't look now, but that guy is Chico; he's the pimp who I left when I met you. Marlon said, "Come on, let's tell my sisters and my brother to get out of here." Chico heard Marlon call me Kim. Chico said to Marlon, "Hell no!

Her name is not Kim. She told me that her name is Kamiah." Marlon said, "Don't answer him. Just keep on moving." We rushed and started to run out in a hurry to find his siblings. Mary and John said, "Hey, Wait you guys. What's going on?" We hurried out of the house to get to the car and Marlon yelled back to his friend's John and Mary, "I'll call you later."

When we left, Marlon yelled out loud, "Man! Somebody flattened all the tires on my car." Suddenly, several guys came toward us swirling around long heavy chains in the air. They were trying to hit us with them.

We ran two blocks away from them. to get to the main highway. By the time we got there, we looked back they were gone. We ran another block to get to the signal light! Our hearts were beating fast, we were breathing so hard. A car drove up and it stopped at the red light. Marlon grabbed the handle of the man's car door to open it. We jumped into his car. Marlon and I got into the front seat with this oriental man.

The Oriental man looked to be in his late forties. His eyes got so big they were bulging like the size of two saucers. (LOL) Marlon said, "Man this is an emergency. Please take us to Los Angeles. We will pay you. It's a gang chasing us." The man gripped the steering wheel with two hands. He leaned his chest forward close to the steering wheel. Marlon said, "Man speed it up." With the oriental man's accent, he said, "No, I get ticket," We all said to him in unison. "Then you can tell the police about the guys chasing us." The man sped off as fast as he could. The tires squealed as they burned rubber. There was no policeman in sight.

We were safe and on our way home. We looked behind to see if anyone was following us. Thank God, we had ditched them. We really got back to Marlon's home fast. It seemed like it took us only about 15 minutes to get there. It would usually take us 25 minutes to get to L.A. from San Pedro.

As soon as we arrived at the house, Marlon and his brother gave the man some money. The oriental man was so happy to drop us off. He had a big smile on his face. When he realized we weren't going to harm him, he kept smiling as he drove away. When we got out of the car we burst out laughing. We laughed so hard about when we first got into his car. His eyes got big as saucers.

We laughed so hard until our sides were hurting. I had tears in my eyes too, but not from being sad, it was because it was so funny. We could hardly talk just from so much laughter. We tried to imitate the oriental man's eyes by pushing the skin around our eyes with our fingers trying to make them slanted like his. We must have laughed about an hour or so after we got back home.

I was happy that Marlon let me to stay there with him and his family. They were so kind to me. They helped me get away from the pimp Chico. When I ran away with Chico, I got into more trouble than I'd expected. I do believe God sent an angel (Marlon) to bail me out of that bad situation. We all learned a life time of lessons. What lesson did I learn when I left home with Chico? Never go anywhere with a stranger.

Chapter 15

NIGHTCLUB DANCERS IN 1959

I left Los Angeles soon after the gangbangers chased Marlon and me from the Party. I was so glad to be going back home to Santa Monica. I called my sister Venetia as soon as I got there. She answered the phone. I let her know I was coming back home. I gave her directions to the service station, where my baby and I were waiting. It took 10 minutes for her to drive there to pick us up. By the time we got into the car Patricia had fallen asleep. My sister said, "Girl! I'm so glad you're back because your husband was so sad. He got drunk on beer every day. He comes over to our house so drunk!

We told him that we didn't know where you were! He said, he was praying that you'd come back to him! I see God answered his prayer!

My sister said "No matter what happens between you and Harold, you need to keep in touch with the family! We don't need to worry and wonder if you're doing alright. I hope you two stays together this time!"

Venetia, I'll try my best to stay with him, but if he cheats on me again I'm going to file for a divorce. My sister gave me two telephone numbers so I could call my husband. The number was to his job. The other number was his home phone.

First, I called him at his job. The receptionist took my message for him to let him know I was back in town. He can call me at my sister Venetia's home. He has her phone number. Thank you."

While waiting for him to return my call, I help my sister Venetia to prepare dinner. We had barbecue chicken for dinner. The aroma from the food was tantalizing, it filled the air. I seasoned the baked beans with brown sugar and mustard. She had smoked turkey to cook with the turnip greens. She made the potato salad with dill and sweet pickles, onions, red bell pepper, and boiled egg with mustard; it was delicious. The peach cobbler had sugar, lemon juice, cinnamon, nutmeg, and butter with a sweet tart taste. The cobbler had a golden-brown crust. The peach cobbler was so good topped with vanilla ice cream. Yummy! Girl, I'm getting hungry. That sounds good to me.

She said, "This is my husband's favorite dinner. After we feed them we'll ask them to take us out tonight. There's a talent show tonight at the nightclub. They are giving out monetary prizes too. That'll be a fun place to celebrate, you and Harold getting back together, is that okay?" Yeah! I like that idea.

By the time we finished cooking, the telephone rang. So Venetia said, "Answer the phone Kamiah. It's probably for you." Yes, she was right. It was my husband. "Hello." With excitement in his voice Harold said, "Hello Kamiah, I gave Venetia my telephone numbers just the other day. I didn't know we'd be talking this soon. Can I come see you?" Yes! 'm so glad you left your phone number with her; I was hoping we'd talk. He said, "Talk? What do you mean?" Oh! I said, "I do mean talk and be together in person of course."

He said, "Wow! I thought you meant you just wanted to talk. I want to see you first. I'm sure we'll have things to talk about, right? "Yes, you're right." Honey I'll be here at Venetia's waiting for you, okay? I added, by the way we're cooking Erwin's favorite dinner." Harold said, "Baby as soon as I go home, I will take my shower and get dressed, I'll be right over. See you baby."

My husband cheated on me again. I left him for 3 months. But I missed having a family. So I forgave him so we could be a family again. He was excited to hear from me again. Shortly, after I finished talking to him, brother-in-law came in from work. My sister and I had finished decorating the dining room table. My brother-in-law Erwin came into the kitchen and said to his wife, "Hey babe, the aroma smells scrumptious." He gave her a hug and kiss. Next, he said, "Hey sister-in-law, as he tapped me on my head." "I know your husband's going to be glad to see you girl! Does he know you're back in Santa Monica?" "Yes, he knows I'm here. He'll be here shortly.

The doorbell rang. My heart was beating fast. I was just standing there, instead of opening the front door. I ran around in circles in the living room, Venetia looked at me with a stern looks on her face. She had one eyebrow raised. While gritting her teeth, she said, "Answer the door. Why are you standing there? You know you're expecting your husband."

Before I answered the front door, I glanced in the mirror, then I sprayed some cologne behind my ears. I tossed a peppermint candy in my mouth. I was wearing a tight-fitted black mini dress. It had short puffed polka-dotted sleeves with a U-neckline. I had on my sandal strapped black high heel shoes. I took a deep breath as I reached for the door knob and snatched it open.

While he stood on the front porch, he reached for my hand to pull me closer to him. We gave each other a big hug. He swept me off my feet to hold me in his arms, as he whispered in my ear "Baby I missed you." "Honey I missed you too." Before we entered the apartment, we sneaked a kiss. He was looking so handsome to me. The cologne he wore had a romantic scent. It was a mild scent crossed between chocolate with mints. Wow! he smelt good. He was wearing a black leisure suit with black Stacy Adam shoes. He wore his hair processed. After we entered the apartment he was still standing and holding me in his arms. He said, "Hey sister-in-law, how's it going? Where's Erwin?"

She said, "I'm doing great. Erwin is in the room getting dressed." By the time my husband put me down my brother-in-law walked into the living room. He said, "How's everything brother-in-law?" "Everything is going great now." He said with a big smile on his face, my baby is home.

By the time we sat down Venetia said, "Okay you all, dinner is ready." Harold said,

"Sister-in-law the dinner looks good, smells good, and I know it's going to taste good too." Erwin said, "Man I know my wife can cook." Erwin said the blessing over the food and we began eating. It was less talking and plenty of humming with every bite of food, it was so delicious. My sister said, "Okay you guys, since we prepared your favorite dinner; we need you guys to take us to the nightclub tonight, okay?" "Yeah, you ladies deserve to go out. Thanks for cooking the delicious dinner.

Venetia said, "We'd like to go to the club tonight, okay you guys." Erwin said, "I thought it was a catch why you cooked a big delicious dinner. It's in the middle of the week." He laughed jokingly, ha, now that I've eaten. He rubbed his belly and yawned, using a squeaky singing falsetto voice, he said, "I could go lie down and go to sleep. I'm full now." Erwin was trying to get us to laugh and he succeeded. We laughed so hard until our stomachs hurt and tears filled my eyes. While Harold was still laughing he said to Erwin, "come on man, stop the bull…and let's take our beautiful ladies out tonight. They deserve to go to the club. Venetia and I knew how to get dressed in a hurry. When Harold came over; he was already dressed in a nice navy-blue leisure suit. That was when leisure suits were popular. So when Erwin came into the living room he had on his leisure suit too. I was already dressed before my husband got there. I wore a mini length wrap-around dress with a built-in bra. It was strapless. The color was royal blue; for the background, it had three large yellow Hawaiian flowers on it. I wore my black high-heel sandal shoes. Venetia joined us in the living room; my husband said, "Kamiah, did you and Venetia plan to dressed alike?" Venetia said we didn't. But we just think alike and ended up wearing the same outfit I had on. My sister and I had so much in common, that we acted like twins.

It was amazing that our husbands both wore their leisure suits. But they didn't plan it that way, it just happened. We all danced our way to the car doing the cha, cha, cha!

We got into my husband's car, and we were on our way to the club.

We stopped to buy some silver satin wine and cups at the liquor store. We sipped on the wine on our way. As soon as I had a few sips of it I felt tipsy. It didn't take much for me. The nightclub was 10 miles away from where they lived.

It didn't take us long to drive there. I sat in the front seat with my head laid back. I was so tipsy. My husband had to help me out of the car. He said, "Come on out princess, we're here." Venetia and Erwin said, "Kamiah you had too much to drink already. Take it easy! My speech was slow and slurred when I answered them, I said, "SOOO-kay!" As we walked up to the entrance of the club, there was a poster on the wall. It read: "Talent show, win cash prizes."

Venetia leaned close to me whispering in my ear, "Kamiah, remember the dance steps we use to practice." I said, yes. She said, "Let's try out for the talent show; we can do our dance routine, okay?" We signed up for the talent show! We were so excited about it! We were fortunate enough to get a table close to the stage. We were the fifth act on the list. We told our husbands that we had to go to the dressing room to wait for the M.C. to call us. In the meantime, we watched a few people perform. Just before the forth act finished we headed to the dressing room. Then we change into our costumes.

When we heard the band play Latin Music, this was our cue to get ready to come out dancing! The M.C. stepped to the microphone. He said, loud and slow: "Ladies and gentlemen, put your hands together with a big round of applause to welcome Venetia and Vienna. They come all the way from the "Hebbirdy Islands. They are dynamic exotic dancers; performing for the first here in Los Angeles. (My stage name is Vienna, I was 19.) We came out of the dressing room dancing to the beat mambo music; making our entrance. We danced in and out between the tables where the audience was sitting; making our way to the stage.

Our husbands had big smiles on their face as they watched us dance. They applauded and whistled. They were just as enthusiastic as the patrons watched us. I learned how to dance the mambo when I was in the girl's school. I taught my sister how to dance the mambo. She taught me how to do modern dancing. We combined the steps which we created our own style of dancing. The crowd loved it.

The M.C. called for the three winners to come on stage. He called the third-place winner first. Carmichael was the second-place winner. We all applauded for him! He was a great roller skate dancer. The M.C. took his time and teased the audience before he announced the first-place winners. He said it slowly, Ladies and Gentlemen, let's give the winners a big round of applause. Let's welcome the exotic dancers Venetia and Vienna. They are from the Hebbirdy Islands. The crowd roared with a big applause as they gave us a standing ovation.

The band played Latin music as Venetia and I danced the mambo. We danced all the way through the crowded room. We weaved in and out of the crowd as we danced our way to the stage. The M.C. gave us a $125.00 each for the first-place prize. Plus, a contract to dance five nights a week. We danced Wednesday night through Sunday night every week.

Our husbands were happy for us that we won first-place. They were excited to be our body guards too. After we asked them to, the Manager said, "Ladies congratulations! You have the job!

We were happy that our husbands were there to support us. He said, "These are the costumes that our dancer's wear." We wore tiny metallic material circles that covered our nipples with tassels hanging from them.

We bought bikini swim suits to wear on our bottoms. Our husband signed our contracts to confirm that they approved for us to wear the costumes. The owner said, "We're set to go." With big smiles on our husband's face they answered we're here to support our wives. Thanks guys." Our husbands didn't hesitate to agree to be our body guards. All of their drinks and ours were on the house and the owner said, "Thanks guys!

The owner gave us our monetary prizes. It was 2:30 a.m. We were on our way home. After we got into the car our husbands said to us, "we didn't know you two could dance like that. You young ladies are stars now." While we were waiting at the stop light Harold said, "Baby when you learned to dance like that?" I answered, "Honey I learned the Mambo and cha- cha when I was at the Girl's School. Then when I came home Venetia and I would practice dancing together before I met you."

He said, "My mambo baby." I squeezed his hand as I smiled back. By that time the signal light turned green and we proceeded on our way to drop off Erwin and Venetia at their apartment. We lived in Venice which was about a 15 minutes' drive from their place.

We laughed and talked for hours our first day back together after being separated for three months. We were exhausted from a long day but we were happy to be home.

Even though he didn't get much sleep that night, he went to work because promised his boss to train a new driver. He said "Baby since you and your sister don't have to be at the nightclub until 8:00 tonight, get your rest while I go to work. Don't worry about cooking dinner because when I get off from work, we'll go out to dinner. Is that okay?" "Yes honey, that's great."

After he left for work I went back to bed. As soon as I was in the middle of a good sleep the telephone rang. I tried to ignore the phone by putting the pillow over my head hoping to muffle out the noise. The phone kept ringing and ringing. I snatched the pillow off my head and slammed it on the floor. My goodness! Why don't they just hang up.

I answered the phone with an attitude. I said, "Hello! Who- is- it?" My husband said to me, "Baby wait calm down, why are you so upset?" I calmed down. "Honey I'm sorry. I didn't' know it was you." He explained, "Baby it's always wise to answer the telephone in a pleasant voice. It could be the president."

Yes, honey you're right. "Baby the guy I was supposed to train today didn't come in. I decided to take you to lunch. Is that okay with you?" "Honey that will be great." "Baby you'll still have time to rest before you and Venetia go to the club tonight."

It was 10:30 in the morning; as soon as we hung up the phone I took my shower and got dressed so I would be ready when he came to pick me up. At 11:45, I heard a big rubbish truck drive up out front. I looked out the front window and it was him. I opened the door, stood on my tip toes and threw my arms around his neck.

With a big hug, he lifted me up off my feet and said, "Baby you make coming home worthwhile. You're looking good and smell so sweet. Are you sure you want to go to lunch or just stay home?"

"Honey you must be kidding." Then he said, "Do you want to try me?" I said "Honey, we'd better go to lunch because I'm hungry." He responded, "Yeah babe you're right. Let's go eat." We headed off to our favorite seafood restaurant not too far from where we lived. When we got there we decided to order our food to go so we could spend more time alone back at the apartment.

Later on, after work my husband surprised me. I didn't have to cook because we went out for dinner. We went to the same restaurant. To our surprise my sister and her husband were there. By the time the four of us finished dinner, we had 30 minutes before we had to be at the club. It was our first official night as professional dancers.

She whispered in my ear and asked, "Vienna did you bring your costume with you?" "Yes, I have it in my purse" She said, "Good! Yes, I have mine too." Even though my husband had planned that he and I would get a chance to get some rest before going to the club. We didn't worry about missing a little rest because my sister and I were so excited about having our dancing job.

After our husbands paid the waitress we all rushed out of the restaurant to head for the club. Since Venetia and I could only dance when we were tipsy, we had just enough time to stop at the liquor store. We sipped on the wine as Harold was driving us, because we were in a hurry to get to the club on time.

We got to the club early enough to relax and talk with the owner. A few people were there drinking at the bar and listening to the jukebox. My husband said to Erwin, "We got here in time to get a table right up front to keep an eye on our wives." Erwin said, "Yeah man we gotta make sure the guys keep their hands off our wives because they're looking good."

We heard our husband's talking about how they were going to protect us. I said to Venetia, "I'm glad our husbands don't mind being here with us. You know they could've given us a hard time, but they came to watch us dance.

The band started playing music as the patrons were arriving. The first act was a standup comedian. Next there was a guy playing his guitar and sang a blues song. The third act was Carmichael who came out on the stage dancing in roller skates keeping time with the music. He was good.

My sister and I were waiting our turn to go on stage after Carmichael. The first time we danced we went on stage right after him. We went to our dressing room to put on our costumes.

We stayed in the dressing room waiting for the M. C. to call us. Surprisingly, the M.C. didn't call us first, instead he called Big Bobby Mack to sing. He sang a slow romantic song. The ladies were screaming, "Oh sing that song honey." We wanted to see what the crowd was screaming about. But we had to stay out of sight so the patrons couldn't see us in our bikini costumes until it was time. As Big Bobby Mack was closing his song, we could hear the ladies screaming, "Encore, encore, give us more honey."

The master of ceremony said, "Let's give Big- Bobby-Mack another round of applause." He sang the bridge and the last chorus of the song; the ladies were still yelling as he closed his song for the second time. We could hear a lady's voice yelling out to him, "Honey, you can call me anytime." When Big Bobby Mack got to the dressing room he said to us, "I know that fat cow wasn't expecting me to call her." The group of us who were waiting in the dressing room cracked up laughing about his remarks because he had a disgusting look on his face; we asked him, "Was she ugly Big Bobby?"

He said, "h--- yes!" I said to him, "Don't let her spoil your day. She only thinks you're handsome. You made her happy tonight that's all. So, don't take it to heart, she just might give you a big tip." He said, "Yeah, yeah, okay you're right."

This was our first night to dance professional! We had one last sip of silver satin wine to take the edge off being nervous. We touched up our hair and make-up to get ready for the stage. When we heard the band playing the mambo song, we knew we were coming up next. In his enthusiastic deep Baritone voice, the M.C. shouted, Ladies and gentlemen here is the exotic dancing team. Let's welcome them to the stage for their first time, the fabulous Venetia and Vienna from the Hebbirdy Islands.

As the Latin music played we danced from the dressing room through the crowd until we reached the stage. The crowd and our husbands roared with an applause, yelling for us to dance some more. The club was crowded.

They were yelling "Shake that thing baby! We'd do our team dancing and then do our special steps individually. I would do the mambo steps to the rhythm of the Latin music and then I'd shake my shoulders as I went down bending my knees until my shoulders touched the floor.

The next time Venetia joined me. We shook our shoulders and turn our hips at an angle while doing the splits at the same time. The crowd was screaming. "Work it baby, work it." That was a new step to our routine dance that our husbands didn't see us do the first night.

We purposely added new steps to our dance, especially for them because we didn't want to bore them. Every day we'd practice new steps to keep it fresh. We danced five nights a week for 5 months.

We lost interest in our dancing job, but we couldn't figure out why? We were no longer excited about making new costumes. We no longer had the desire to drink Silver Satin wine either. We happened to feel that way at the same time and we didn't know why? My sister said, "Vienna (my stage name) I don't feel like dancing at the nightclub anymore. What about you?" With a frown on my face, I had a lack of interest too.

I was happy that I didn't have to get drunk to dance half-nude. For the first time, I felt ashamed of dancing half-nude.

In the first place, my sister convinced me to dance at the club. When I was 19 she told me to tell the club manager that I was 21. We had no idea of the rumors going around about us dancing half-nude. We didn't know it but our parents had been praying for us to stop dancing.

Our husbands were shocked that we didn't want to dance any longer. Welcome home baby." He grabbed me and gave me a big hug. "I enjoyed every minute you danced, but baby I make enough money to buy all the things you need. Okay?"

I said, "Okay!" I had a sigh of relief, even though I liked to dance. Five nights a week was beginning to be a bit much for me. I was glad that was our last night. We had Monday and Tuesday nights off, and we had enough time to think it over. We decided not to dance half-nude in the nightclub again. Thank God!

We had a good night's sleep. But we stayed in bed until 10:00 that morning. We talked about my short-lived dancing career. He said, "Baby you don't have to dance for money. I'm all you need. It was amazing how my husband was so content with my decision to quit my job. Our husbands were happy to have us home again.

They went to the club every night we danced. They were just as excited as the patrons when we danced. I had no idea that our husbands wanted us to stop dancing. One thing, I liked about my husband, he never pressured me to do anything I didn't want to do. He just let me to make my own decision then he'd agree or disagree.

When we got to the nightclub Erwin and Venetia had arrived a few minutes before us. Erwin made a comment that we needed to go to a music concert. Harold said, "Man you know how it goes, our wives like to dance so we try to make them happy, right?" We all really had a good time dancing. After we left the nightclub we were all tipsy and tired.

Erwin said to us, "Venetia and I are going to see a movie tomorrow, do you guys wanna go with us?" No man, I gotta get some rest so I can go to work on Monday. We kept in touch, but we didn't hang out much any longer.

Chapter 16

FORCED TO DRINK LIQUOR

It was summer and school was out. My sister-in-law whose name is Julie didn't have children of her own. She asked if she could keep my daughter Patricia while she was on vacation from her job. I said, "I'd better check with her dad and see if he will agree for you to keep her." Julie said, "Call me and I'll pick her up."

After my husband came home, he said, babe the dinner sure smells good. I had cooked a meatloaf, mashed potatoes with brown gravy, glazed carrots, and sautéed garlic green beans. We had hot dinner rolls too. He took a quick shower, then the three of us sat at the dinner table to eat dinner. We discussed letting our daughter spend the summer with her Aunt Julie. Harold said, "Let's see what Patricia says about staying with her first." He asked, "Baby cakes do you want to stay with your aunt Julie?"

She said, "Yes!" Her Aunt Julie always did fun things with her whenever they were together. She bought her toys and clothes. In addition, she'd take her to Pacific Ocean Park to ride on the kiddy train and Ferris wheel. She'd bring her neighbor's children to play with her also.

Since I wasn't working I had plenty of free time on my hands. I was bored staying home alone; so went to visit my landlady. I was 22 and Tonya was four years older than me. Before I'd visit her, I'd clean up my apartment. We hung out together three days out of the week. I made sure I'd go home on time to prepare my husband's dinner before he came home from work.

It was in the middle of the week, Tonya and I was sipping on vodka with orange juice. We were having a good time singing. I was sitting in the living room on the long black leather sectional sofa. She had a matching black leather covered bar filled with liquor. Her husband and she liked to party a lot. We sipped our drinks as we listened to the music. I began to get tipsy.

We were fans of Diana Ross and the Supremes'. We wanted to record songs one day, so we'd practice singing their songs all day. I started singing along with the Supremes' record, "Stop in The Name of Love." Those were the days we had records. (LOL)

She said, "I'll start the record over and we'll sing it together. Let's pretend like we are the Supremes!" I had more than one drink of vodka and orange juice. I was getting real tipsy. I was so tipsy I forgot to notice the time to have my husband's dinner ready. While we were enjoying ourselves singing, the doorbell rang. While she answered the door, I sat on the sofa waiting to see who was at the door. She said, "Oh hello, Mr. Gibbon." She invited him in. When he came inside he looked at me right away. By the look on his face I knew he was unhappy. With a stern voice he said, "Come on let's go." I got off the sofa and staggered toward him. When I stood next to him, he held my arm with a firm grip! He marched me straight to our apartment. We lived two doors away from the Landlady's place. As soon as we entered our apartment he gave me a push into the living room. I sat on the edge of the sofa.

He went into the kitchen opened the cabinet and pulled out a fifth of liquor. He took the cap off the bottle and gave it to me. With an angry look on his face he drew the gun out of his coat pocket. He pointed it at my head. He said, "You like to drink huh." He pushed the whiskey bottle up to my mouth, saying, take it. Gritting his teeth, as he said, "Go ahead, drink it all." I was taking longer to drink it than he wanted. So he pushed the bottle of whiskey against my mouth real hard. He spoke in a rough tone. He was gritting his teeth. "I said drink it all." The barrel of the hand gun pressed against my forehead.

I knew he wasn't playing with me. I didn't hesitate to do as he commanded me to do. I gulped down the whiskey in a hurry. I was terrified that he would shoot me. I wasn't thinking that the whiskey could have killed me too. I didn't understand why he wanted to kill me. I only had a few drinks with our landlady. It really didn't make sense to me.

After drank most of the fifth of whiskey, I lost my vision I couldn't see him any longer. It felt like the room was spinning around. I was afraid. Within minutes I heard ringing in my ears. I heard his footsteps leaving, as he walked out the front door!. He slammed the door as he left.

He left me to die. Soon after he left I said, Jesus help me! Instantly, I heard a soft voice saying, "Take your fingers and gag yourself." After I gagged myself, I began to vomit whiskey up in abundance.

My cousin answered the telephone, "Arlene, I need you and your husband to come get me right away. "What's wrong are you okay? No, I'm not. I'll tell later when you get here. I can't talk now, I'm using my neighbor's telephone. I was pacing the floor and looking out the window. It took them fifteen minutes to get there.

Arlene said, "Kamiah, what happened? Why are you leaving your husband?" As I started to talk, I began crying as my body shook feeling woozy from the liquor. I told her, "Harold tried to kill me." Even though Arlene heard me clearly, she repeated what I said. He tried to kill you. She couldn't believe what she had just heard, so she said in a louder voice, "Harold did what?"

It was hard for me to answer her. I cried after each word I spoke. I was trying to explain what happened to me. I said, He. I couldn't talk. I cried again. He held a gun to my head. He told me. I tried talking again, he forced me to drink a fifth of liquor. I was so terrified, thinking he'd find me and try to kill me. Thank God, I didn't die from drinking the whiskey. My cousin said, "Kamiah I heard you the first time. But it's so hard to believe Harold would want to kill you.

Still in shock! I thought, what a coward he was forcing me to drink a fifth of liquor. I kept crying. I could've died. I was sitting in the back seat of my cousin's car. She turned around from the front seat to touch my hand to calm me down. "Kamiah, I believe you."

My cousin referred me to her attorney so I could file for divorce. "We'll stop by my house and call to make an appointment." It seemed like everything was working in my favor; the attorney's office he could see me that same day.

Chapter 16a - Divorcing Gibbon

Arlene and her husband drove me to my appointment with the attorney that day. His office was in Culver City. He was plump with a beer belly, standing 5ft 5" tall, dressed in a dark brown suit. He had his glasses sitting on the edge of his nose, while writing something on a paper. He stopped writing as he gazed into space. With his hand under his chin and elbow on the desk he said, "Mrs. Gibbon how long have you been married?" "Twelve years."

"Has your husband ever hit you?" No! "You're still young; why do you want a divorce?" Instead of answering him, I sat there and cried. He was trying to be understanding; so, he asked, "Will you be willing to get counseling?" I slammed my fist on the armrest of the plush chair, and said, "No, counseling won't work for me." He sat up straight in his seat from a leaning position. He bent his head down to glance over the frames of his eyeglasses. "What did he do so bad that you won't give him another chance?" In dismay, I explained, my husband tried to kill me.

After I answered him, I covered my face with my hands. I wept so hard I could barely talk. He gave me some Kleenex to wipe my tears. As I sighed and said, "He held a gun to my head and demanded me to drink a fifth of liquor straight. I raised my voice and screamed, I almost died."

"How long ago did that happen?" It happened this afternoon just before I came in to see you. As he listened to me tell the story, he rocked back and forth vigorously in his plush chair. When I told him, my husband tried to kill me, his eyes stretched open as big as two saucers. He snatched off his eyeglasses. His mouth flew opened in shock. He stuttered as he said, "Mrs. Gibbon "Wait! Calm down! I've heard enough. "Your request for a divorce is granted."

He didn't hesitate to file for my divorce. "Mrs. Gibbon are you feeling better now?" I answered him, "Yes sir I feel much better, thank you." He shook my hands and said, "I'll see you in court in two weeks." "Yes sir, "I responded.

The attorney gave me his business card, and said. "If for any reason you can't make it to your court date, please give me a call." I stayed with my cousin Arlene while waiting for my court date.

While staying with my cousin she asked me to cook for her. She said she liked my cooking. I cooked a delicious Broccoli and sausage casserole for dinner for them; the. ingredients I had were sautéed Italian sausages, cooked rice, garlic, onions, and stewed tomatoes with broccoli spears. I melted cheddar cheese on top. I baked a large pan of golden brown corn bread with melted butter on top. We had a garden salad and a strawberry cool aid drink. I bought readymade shortbread cakes; I served them with fresh sliced strawberries. I topped the cakes with vanilla ice cream with whipped cream for dessert. Yummy! It's making me hungry right now.

My cousin said she never cooked a casserole! "'My family is used to your cooking but they better enjoy it while you're here." After dinner, they all said, "Cous this dinner is delicious! She asked me to give her the recipes before I left! It made me feel good that I could help her. She was a big help to me also. I could relax after the traumatic situation I went through.

Every day I stayed with them they left it up to me to plan the meals. I really didn't mind because I enjoyed their company. They kept me laughing every day. The morning of my court day I was getting anxious. I had to remind myself to breathe deep and exhale slowly, and then I'd relax.

I left my cousins house early, so, I could catch the city bus. I was on my way to the attorney's office. After boarding the bus, I gazed out the window wondering where will I live after my divorce. Tears rolled down my cheeks. I didn't have a job but saved just enough money to pay for my divorce, which was $250.00. (1962)

The sun was shining bright, but it was a gloomy day for me. I arrived at the court building and entered the lobby; I noticed my attorney sitting on a bench near the entrance. He was writing on a document. I walked over to him and smiled. Good morning, Attorney Smith. His briefcase was on his lap. He offered to shake hands with me as he remained seated. "Please have a seat. Mrs. Gibbon I need to complete a few items on your divorce documents before you take the stand to testify.

After completing the documents, he asked, "Do you have future?" I'd like to go back to school to graduate, and get my diploma. "That's a smart thing to do! I wish you all the best." We shook hands, and he said, "You have a restraining order against him now, and he's not allowed to come near you. Does that make you feel better? With tears in my eyes, I nodded my head yes. The attorney continued to say, if he approaches you trying to woo you back don't fall for it! He's a dangerous man! He tried to kill you once, and he might try it again!" Call the police and run to safety!

Chapter 16b - 1962, Filed For A Divorce

Will the case of "Gibbon vs. Gibbon" please take the stand? The Judge asked me to state my full name, Kamiah Gibbon. "Do you solemnly swear to tell the truth and nothing but the truth so helps you God?" "I do."

Since Harold didn't respond to the subpoena the first time, the judge called for him again. The court guard called for him to verify if he had showed up. There was no response from him, the Judge called the court back to order and resumed with my case.

I was so relieved that my trial was over. I was a happy to be leaving my abusive husband. I left the court room feeling happy. I went to the first telephone booth to call my cousin. She and her husband came to pick me up. I knew she didn't have enough room for me to live at her house. So I called a friend of mine.

Chapter 17

SUICIDE ATTEMPT

My friend Janice Mae told me about a man who owned rental property. The rent for his apartments is reasonable, except I didn't have a job. She told me, "He is such a nice man and the reason why I know is, because he gave another friend of mine a break on her rent. She paid only the amount she could afford. He even helped her get a job and I know he'll do the same for you."

I gave Mr. Osteen a call to let him know I was unemployed. I met with him at the apartment and he asked, "What kind of work do you do?" I did domestic work. I was a maid at the Malibu Motel in Malibu, California for a year." So he said that's great, I can help you get plenty of work. As we walked around in the apartment, I asked him, "How much is this apartment renting for?" Mr. Osteen said, "It's $75.00 a month. How much can you pay?" I can pay $25.00 a month to start with."

"I'll be able to help you on one condition and that is nobody else can live here with you." Mr. Osteen showed me the rental agreement. I signed it. We shook hands and he said, "I'll be around to check on you at least once a week to see how you are doing, okay?" I agreed with him and he left.

I saw a lady coming from her house next door to my apartment. She was a tall lady with a beautiful smile. She said, "Good evening young lady, my name is Odessa and yours?" I'm please to meet you Odessa, my name is Kamiah.

She welcomed me to the neighborhood, and offered me to visit her anytime. She asked, "Would you like to come see my garden I planted a few months ago?" "Yes, I'd love to see it." We walked to the back yard to look. I met her children who were playing in the yard on the opposite side of the garden. They were happy to meet me; they asked did I have children. Yes, I do, but they live with their grandparents right now.

After Odessa and I had finished talking she went home and I returned to my place. I was watching television when I heard a key rattling at the door. I turned my television down so I could listen closely to the noise. Then I saw it opening slowly. My heart was beating fast. I was frightened. So I tip toed quickly to the bathroom and locked the door.

I forgot to turn the television off. I didn't hear any more noise so I thought it was safe to come out of the bathroom. I picked up the toilet plunger to use as a weapon in case I needed it (LOL) Then I eased the door open slowly to see if anyone was there. Since it was a bachelor's apartment it didn't take me long to go from one room to another. Since I didn't see anybody come in my apartment, I went to Odessa's house. She said, "Kamiah you look worried what's bothering you?"

I shared with Odessa about Mr. Osteen that he agreed to rent me the apartment for $25.00 a month. I even explained to him that I wasn't working. When he came over today, he said, since he was doing me a favor, I owe him one. Odessa told me that I didn't have to stoop that low. She knew he meant he wanted sexual favors. I said, I'd rather move than to get involved with him sexually.

She said, "Oh no! You don't have to stoop that low to have a place to live. How would you like to live with me and my family?" I don't know how long it will be before I can get a job. I don't want to bother you and your family."

I thanked Odessa for inviting me to live with her. She was kind to me. I told her that I'd be alright and was going to spend the night in my apartment that night. When I went to my apartment before I went to bed, I pushed the sofa bed against the front door so he couldn't unlock the door again. After I went to sleep, every time I heard a noise I would wake up because I'm a light sleeper.

I woke up yawning and stretching as I look at the morning sun light shining through the mini-blinds. I could hear birds chirping outside the window. I was so sleepy because of tossing and turning all night. I worried about not having a job and him coming to harass me about sexual favors. I thought about how my parents didn't want me to come back home.

I was tired of trying to be independent and trying to be an adult. I called home, "Mother can I come back home?" "No! You made your bed hard, now lay in it." Those words cut through my heart as if someone had stabbed me with a butcher knife. When Harold tried to kill me, I didn't want to tell my parents because they never wanted me anyway.

Odessa said, "I don't understand why your parents don't want you?" I started to weep; I was unable to answer her. Odessa moved a chair near the door so I could get some fresh air. She held my hand and said, "Kamiah baby, go ahead and cry, if it will help. I know you must be hurt but let me share something with you, okay?"

When she said she had something to share with me, it really got my attention. I stopped crying. I listened. "Kamiah, I know who really loves you!" I didn't say a word. I waited to hear who loved me.

She said, "Don't you want to know who it is that loves you?" "I am waiting for you to tell me who it is? "God loves you! He cares about all the pain you went through."

I really didn't understand how she knew that God loved me. I asked, "Odessa how do you know He loves me?" "It says it in the Bible, "For God so loved the world, that he gave his only begotten Son, that whosoever believeth in him should not perish but have everlasting life." (John 3:16)

She let me know I could stay with her, but I didn't to because I didn't have money to pay her rent. I was missing my family, but I knew my parent didn't want me back home. I felt so sad that I couldn't take care of myself financially. I didn't want to stay with her for free either.

She invited me to help her prepare the dinner for Thanksgiving Day. I chopped the celery and onions. She cooked cornbread to make the stuffing out of it. I didn't mind helping her because she was such a nice person. While we were preparing the vegetables she said, "I'd like to share some of my story with you if you don't mind." "Please do, I'd love to hear about your life."

I was so traumatized after my husband tried to kill me. It was hard for me to go to sleep at night.

After tossing and turning all night, it was the dawning of a new day. The bright sun light was shining through the sheer drapes. I still hadn't come up with a solution of how to support myself financially. Aw! I thought, I'll just drink the last four cans of beer in the refrigerator which will get me drunk and I'll turn the oven on full blast! I'll go to sleep and never wake up again! Wow! I thought. The best solution was to end my life because no one cared about me any way. I thought again as I began to drink a can of beer. I got a small note pad and pen and began writing:

Dear Dad and Mom:
You didn't want me, you sent me away to a girl's school. My husband tried to kill me. By the time you read this letter you'll be happy to know you don't have to worry about me anymore. I just ask one favor of you. Please love my two babies Michael and Patricia. Please tell them that I wasn't a bad girl because Mrs. Miller told me that I was a good girl, and that is what I believe. I love you.

Sincerely,
your daughter,
Kamiah Gibbon

I wrote that suicide letter, after I guzzled down two more beers. Alligator tears ran down my face. I was about to open my fourth can of beer, but I was so tipsy until every time I lifted the can of beer to my mouth

I'd spill it. I set the can of beer on the floor next to the sofa. I lied down and covered up to go to sleep. I had turned the oven on full blast waiting to die. I hoped that I'd continue to sleep and never wake up.

I was trying to end my life, but I heard a banging noise at the front door! Bang! Bang! Bang! I thought I was dreaming, but the banging kept getting louder and louder. I lied back down to sleep in my clothing. I heard Odessa calling me! "Kim! Kim! She vigorously knocked on the door.

I rolled off the sofa to the floor with my hair was messy. Next, I reached for the arm of the sofa to pull myself up. Then I staggered to open the door. Odessa put her hand over her nose as she entered my apartment. She said, "Kim come on outside! Hurry! I smell gas awfully strong. There's too much gas fumes in your apartment. Let's go to my house. She called the Paramedics to make sure I was alright.

I was so tipsy my legs were wobbly when I walked. I slurred my words as I answered her. I said, "I'm-m o-ka-y." I was ashamed because I tried to end my life. Immediately Odessa's mouth flew wide open. She made a gasping noise as she covered her mouth. She stared in dismay as she wrapped her arms around me. She said, "Kamiah what's wrong?"

We walked a short distance to her house. She told me to, "Inhale and exhale slowly." As soon as we got to her house I sat near the opened window for fresh air. She called the Paramedics. They were there so fast. They checked my vital signs. After I got some fresh air, I was doing just fine. The fumes from the oven were so strong. The paramedic inspectors said it could've killed me. They had to wear gas masks to investigate my apartment. They found where the gas fumes were coming from. But there were no flames in the oven.

The paramedic asked me, "Did you know that the gas was turned on without it being lit?" I didn't want to tell him that I tried to take my life. I answered, "No I didn't know it wasn't lit. He asked, "Do you live alone?" "Yes, I live alone. "He asked, "Do you have someone you can stay with tonight?" "Yes, I have a place to stay." I thought about Odessa inviting me to spend a few nights with her.

"You're invited to Thanksgiving Dinner at our place. I accepted her invitation. I didn't have anywhere else to go. Wow! I said to Odessa, "Yes, thank you, I'd love to join you and your family for dinner." Odessa called her four daughters who were in their bedrooms to come out and set the dining room table. I helped the girls set the table and she said, "Oh no, you're our guest so just relax and enjoy. As I write this story, I can see that it was God who worked through Odessa to come to my rescue. That's why I titled this book "Angels Protected Me."

Chapter 18

OLDER MAN RELATIONSHIP

It was disgusting, when Mr. Osteen wanted me to exchange free rent for sex. It was not an option for me. I wouldn't dare stoop that low. I went to a pay phone to call my friend Marlon. I hadn't seen him in four years. I met him when I was 18 years old, but his brother Leonard answered the phone. He said he was out of town. I asked Leonard if I could come to stay at their house because I had nowhere to go. He said, "Marlon would return in two weeks and he couldn't let me stay without his permission. I took a chance to find another friend. I walked Ben's' house who lived a block away from Marlon.

I rode the city bus to his house was on McKinley Avenue and 40th Place in Los Angeles. By the time I arrived, Leonard was gone. I remembered, Mr. Bernard was their landlord who lived in the back house. So I went there.

I rang the doorbell to see if Mr. Bernard was home. He opened the door. Hello, my name is Kamiah. Do you remember me? "Your face looks familiar but I don't remember the name." He didn't know me by Kamiah because the last time I saw him, Marlon introduced me as "Kim."

It had also been four years since I saw him. I asked, "Do you remember me as Kim?" That is when he laughed and said, "Yes, Kim is the name I remember." With a big grin on his face, he invited me to come in. He was a tall, slim, a gray-headed distinguished man. He was part Afro-American and French. He wore a black patch over his left eye. He said, "What brings you out this time of night to visit me?" "I need a place to stay. Do you have any vacancies for rent? He answered, "Yes I do have a vacancy." "May I see the apartment tonight?"

We were standing in the living room of his home. He led me down a small hallway, he opened the door to show me the bedroom. He said, "This bedroom is for rent but only to you. Is that okay with you?" Yes, but where is your wife? He said, he and his wife had been divorced for four years.

I'm sorry to hear that you and you wife are divorced. Then he said, "No don't feel sorry. The divorce was the best thing that ever happened to me." But, I thought, he and his wife was happy when they were together.

Ms., "tomorrow, I will write the rules out for you to sign. Okay?" As I signed the agreement, I told him that I was bringing my daughter to live with me.

He said "Oh that's alright, I'd love to meet her. After I brought my daughter there I was hoping to live with him just long enough until I got a job. But after, we sipped on some tequila margarita cocktails, we got tipsy. Out of the clear blue, he said, "Kim you can sleep with me and forget about paying the rent." Think about it? I told him, I wouldn't have sex with him unless he married me.

He smiled as he touched my hand. We were sitting on the same sofa. It was a long sectional sofa. The color was tan, and the carpet was a chocolate brown. He said, "I'd like to get to know you." You'll be glad you did, If you let me be a part of your life and be your only man."

He said, "You'll be glad if you give me a chance to love you." When he said those words that really touched my heart. I thought to myself; he wants a chance to love me. I thought wow! That's great! He was thirty years older than me and he didn't talk to me like most guys around my age. I took an interest in him and took him serious. He'd take me places I'd never been. I never knew that I'd go back on my word of not exchange rent for sexual favors. I didn't find a job yet. Plus, I had nowhere to go. I reneged on my word, then I said, okay I'll be your lady. That was the beginning of our relationship. I learned to be content with giving him a chance to love me. He taught me how to cook his favorite dishes.

One day, my sister Venetia called me. She was leaving her husband. She asked could she live with us. We were running buddies most of our life. I was happy to let her stay with me. We had a lot in common. We were like twins. We are both musicians. We like to sing, and we are both artist too.

Chapter 19

TERRIFIED BY SKELETONS

It was a hot summer day, in 1963, when my sister Venetia came to live with me. She said she had broken up with her husband. She shared the bedroom with my daughter. After a week, we enrolled in a singing class at night. We were learning to sing secular songs. When we were home with our parents we could only sing gospel songs.

The first song I learned to sing was "Sunny Yesterday My Life Was Filled with Rain." The instructor liked the way I sang it, so, he asked me to sing a duet with a young man. He sang baritone voice and I sang soprano. We rehearsed that song for two weeks. The instructor was impressed with our performance! So, he gave us another song to learn. It was "On a Clear Day," which was going to be our next assignment for the following week.

On our way home, my sister said, "Our parents raised us to sing gospel so and they'll object if we sing secular songs. She said, "The LORD spoke and told me to stop singing secular songs. We've got to stop singing those kinds of songs. I said, "The LORD didn't speak to me. If you want to stop singing secular songs go ahead." We had only been singing in the class for a month. I really enjoyed singing. As a matter of fact, I expected to become a recording artist.

Then she said, "You know when our parents prayed for us and the Holy Spirit convicted us to stop dancing. Now I feel the same Holy Spirit tugging at my heart again." I said, "I don't see anything wrong with singing these songs. In a stern voice she said, "Girl we have to get out of this singing class because I heard from God. She told me that Jesus is coming back again and we might go to hell." But she wanted me to stop singing because she said, she heard from God. I only stopped because I wanted her to be quiet and leave me alone. I decided to go back to church with her to see if she was right.

We went to church for a while and things were going well for us. She enjoyed going to church more than I did. Listening to biblical stories over and over was boring to me. I didn't know how to relate to them. I stopped going to church. She would call to tell me that it takes time to understand the Bible. She asked, "How can you learn what the Bible says without being taught by a preacher?"

I really didn't understand what she was talking about. When I walked away from church I knew I didn't walk away from God because I pray daily. I read my Bible daily. Since she wanted to stop going to the nightclubs I didn't feel the same way. I wanted her to leave me alone and go her own way. She felt the spirit tugging at her, not me. She got me to thinking, if I was singing the right songs to please God.

I gave my third oldest sister Rhonda a call and asked her if she would babysit for me. We drove from Los Angeles to Santa Monica to take my daughter to her house. We stopped by Venetia's lady friend's house since we were in the area. She had been going to church three months longer than me. While I was driving to her friend's house, she said, she changed her mind about going to church. She said, "I believe we can go back to the nightclub as long as we don't get drunk.

Venetia is two years older than me, and she usually convinces me to see things her way. When I was 19 and she was 21, she persuaded me to dance in the nightclub. She told me to tell the manager that I was 21, but it wasn't true.

I was excited, when we went back to the nightclub again. Going to church was so square to me anyway. I asked her, "Why were you so positive that we would go to hell? Now you think it's alright to go back to the nightclub?" She said, "Girl we're not going there to dance in little costumes like we did before, that's what makes it different this time. I know

God understands we're just going out to have fun. So don't worry we'll be alright." I asked her to make up her about being a Christian? She was confusing me about her religious beliefs.

When Friday came I told Mr. Bernard that we were going to the nightclub. He said, "I don't mind you going out. Just be careful and don't stay out past 2:00 a.m., okay?" I assured him that we'd be in early. He knew I liked to dance and he didn't like going out. He wanted me to have fun as long I came home before the sun came up.

She said, "Sis you got it made. He lets you go out without him. My husband never lets me go out alone." We had new outfits to wear. We liked to dress alike. We liked it when people asked were we twins? We'd tell them yes. We dressed up in our black low cut, spaghetti straps, mini length dresses. We wore matching black high heel shoes with rhinestones. It was time for us to go out and have a good time. We thought we were looking glamorous!

Venetia left her husband to come stay with me because she caught him cheating. She told me, "I'm gonna find a tall dark handsome man to date. So I can get even with him." I told her that was the wrong thing to do because she might get with a crazy man. We drove away in my little red Corvette to the nightclub. She complained all the way about her husband cheating. She kept saying how she'd get even with him. I told her, if she did she might end up being sorry. I asked, do you really think that trying to get even will make it right? What if you get pregnant with the other man?" Then, she said, "That'll never happen to me because I have the secret to keep from getting pregnant. I'll cross that bridge when I get to it."

We parked in front of the Nightclub. Before we went in I said, "Sis you're not making sense saying you'll have to cross that bridge when you get there. The reason why is, you're getting another man involved with your life. You don't know if he'll be in love with you? I kept silent because I wasn't getting anywhere arguing. She snatched her purse and folded her arms as she stared out the window. She was angry. She screamed and snapped at me as she said, "This is my life. I can do whatever I want. When she said that to me, I remembered our mother taught me a Scripture when I was five years old. It was Proverbs 15:1 says, "A soft answer turns away wrath but grievous words stir up anger."

So I decided to be quiet. I quoted the scripture in my mind while she screamed at me. When she noticed I wasn't responding; she began to calm down. She said, "Come on let's go in and find somebody to dance with." When I kept quiet she stopped arguing. "Okay, we might as well go in the club since we're here."

We went into the nightclub and paid the $5.00 cover charge to the doorman. He asked, "Did you young ladies come alone?" "Yes, we did!" Is it okay?" Then the young man said, "Just be careful because there are some strange guys in this club. You may not come out the same way you went in."

We didn't question him we paid our fee and walked to the other side of the burgundy curtain. As soon as we entered on the other side I couldn't believe my eyes! I rubbed my eyes and then I bugged my eyes. I grabbed my sister's hand. I was terrified when I saw skeletons in the nightclub.

"Do you see what I saw?" She said, "Are you talking about that skeleton sitting at the organ playing it and smoking a cigarette? I can see smoke traveling down and up through its bones. We saw the skeletons dancing on the floor!" There's never been a time in my dreams that I saw anything like that. We knew it was real life. Get this. We weren't dreaming about skeletons. That happened to us in real life. We were wide awake when we saw the skeletons dancing.

It was frightening to see skeletons dancing. We grabbed each other's hand as we hurried out the door. We whispered at the same time: LET'S GET OUT OF HERE." That was something we'd never experience in our lives before. We knew it was God showing us the spiritual world of darkness. We knew our parents prayed for us and God was letting us know we didn't need to be in the nightclubs.

When we got outside, we got into the car, locked the doors, and sped away. I said, "God surely sent us a message that we'll never forget. It was weird and scary too, to see skeleton's dancing. The skeleton at the organ played the most beautiful music I've ever heard." But I was terrified.

Venetia said, "Girl I'm so glad we didn't drink any booze because we could've turned into skeletons also." I answered "Yeah! Thank God we didn't take any liquor." I think God was showing us that death takes over a person's life in the nightclubs. The doorman was trying to warn us before we entered the club! No, we didn't question him because we thought we were looking cute and thought he was trying to make a pass at us.

As I sped down the highway, I didn't pay attention to the speed limit. We were so afraid and desperate to get home. Venetia said, "Vienna [my stage name] you need to slow down. It was seconds after Venetia told me to slow down, the Policeman pulled me over. I looked in the rearview mirror. Sure, enough there were red lights flashing behind my car. She said, "See! I told you to slow down."

I was already shaking up over the skeletons, so I screamed at Venetia, "OH! Shut up!" I pulled over to the curb. I rolled down the window waiting for the officer to write me a ticket. That was my first time to get a traffic violation ticket. I was so nervous my hands were sweaty and shaky. I began crying.

The Officer came to the driver's door; he shined a flashlight in my face. He asked to see my driver's license. "How fast were you driving?" I answered "Sir, I believe I was going 35 MPH." Before he said anything else, he walked back to his car. I looked over at my sister, there was another officer questioning her.

The assistant officer said, "Ladies step out of the car until we search it." "Have you young ladies been drinking?" "NO Sir." "Young lady, your driving record is cleared. I'll give you a warning this time. Remember to slow down. Next time you'll get a ticket. Is that clear?" "Yes Sir."

Wow! Thank God! I didn't get a ticket. Our parents must be praying for us again. As the officer walked away, I realized he didn't have to be nice. I drove off slowly heading for home. Venetia said, "Sis, I'm sorry I talked you into going to the nightclub. Now I know that we need to get back in Church." I said to her, "We need to read our Bibles also."

We were so happy to get home; it was still in the early part of the night. We rushed into the house and I picked up the Bible off the night stand and began reading. I fell on my knees and cried out to God saying, "Father God, please forgive us for going to the nightclub, I pray in Jesus' name, Amen!"

Later that night around 11:30 p.m., I was getting ready for bed when I heard the front door open. It was Big Richard coming from work. He said, "Kim I thought you and your sister would still be at the club.

Are you feeling okay?" I answered, "If I told you what happened you may not believe what we saw." So, he said, "Why don't you give it a try, tell me what happened." I called my sister to join us in the living room so we both could tell him together what we saw. With excitement, we began telling him in unison about the dancing skeletons. The strange thing about it is that we were not dreaming. I am so glad that Venetia was there to be my witness. It was weird to see skeletons moving around.

He laughed and said, "I think somebody spiked your drinks. You girls were probably hallucinating and imagined that you saw skeletons. So, I said "See! I knew you wouldn't believe us. He said, "How on earth could you see skeletons moving? Don't you know skeletons don't have life?"

He said, for skeletons to move they need flesh on their bones, blood inside the flesh, and they need to breathe! He sarcastically said, "Who do you think is going to believe you." One thing I knew for sure was there is nothing impossible for God to do. He got our attention. I believe that was the work of the Lord to give us a warning to stay away from the nightclubs. Okay have it your way. He walked away in disbelief of the episode.

Since he didn't understand about the spiritual world of light and the spiritual world of darkness, it was difficult for him to perceive our experience. He shook his head in disbelief. He looked at me like I was crazy. If my sister had not witnessed the skeletons with me, I imagine we would've been in disbelief too. Wow! That was one experience in my life that I'll never forget. I hope I'll never see it again.

I never want to go to another nightclub. That was the worst nightclub experience I've had. I found a job and bought a car. I opened a savings account, because I didn't like being in a common law relationship. When I told him, I wanted to get married, he was against it. He said "No! I'll never put my thumb under the hammer again."

Chapter 20

EXPECTING MY THIRD CHILD

Now, I was 26 years old. I made plans to live alone. But I didn't realize I was pregnant until I missed two periods. I thought about having an abortion, but I was afraid. I really didn't know what to do.

My mother told me that having an abortion is a sin. I was ashamed and thought about the fact that my baby didn't have a choice in the matter!. Since I was the one who made the mistake of getting pregnant, I took full responsibility to care for my child. I thank God that I didn't get an abortion. I thank God for my adorable son. He is a gift from heaven. As a matter of fact, I thank God for my four children.

After I told him that I was pregnant he had a proud look on his face. Whatever food I had a taste for he'd buy it. I'd craved homemade hamburgers. I had lettuce, tomato, onions, avocado slices, and Dill pickles with miracle whip dressing on a sesame seed hamburger bun. I had an ice-cold Dr. Pepper soda to drink. Yummy! I can taste it now.

While living with him, I started going to church. I wanted him to go with me so he could learn about the importance of marriage. I expected him to marry me since I was pregnant. I didn't like shacking up because it's a sin. Since there was no hope in getting him to marry me, I decided to stay with him until the baby was born.

After my six months checkup, the doctor found out I had toxemia in my blood. The doctor advised me to have a caesarean section. He assured me that the procedure would be best for us. I was afraid of the idea, but I remembered to pray, and I kept busy.

Finally, my 9th month came; it was May 25th and I was feeling so energetic that day. I had prepared a hearty lunch. After eating, I felt like cleaning the house. It was dinner time and I was still working. Mr. Bernard said, "Kamiah after all that work you've done you must be getting hungry again? I said, "I'm doing okay." He said, "You've done enough work, get rest before you go into labor. I smiled and said, "I'm okay.

I sat down to relax. I had worked up an appetite, but I couldn't figure out what I wanted to eat. I made a meatloaf sandwich with Dill pickles; it was delicious. A few hours after dinner, I relaxed in the bathtub. I could feel my baby move in my stomach to a new position. It was 9th month; I expected to go to the hospital any day. It was after nine o'clock that night when I got in bed. I couldn't find a comfortable position, so I tossed and turned a while.

I rolled up a pillow to put it under my leg while I laid half way on my side. Shortly after I went to sleep, the labor pains woke me up. I looked at the clock it was only 12:30 a.m.; I was so sleepy. But it was time for me to go to the hospital. The labor pains were getting close together. I woke up Mr. Bernard. He jumped out of bed in a hurry. It didn't take us to get ready to go to the hospital. Since it was 12:30 a.m. my daughter Patricia was in her bedroom asleep. We let her stay home while we took the 30-minute drive to the County General Hospital.

The nurse checked my vital signs and helped me change into a gown. She rolled me into the labor room. But my pains weren't close enough together for the baby to be born. After two, the nurse checked my blood pressure. It was too high. So she gave me an injection to induce the labor.

Wow! I had severe labor pains. The female doctor reached inside my uterus with her hand in a rubber glove. I could feel her poking and pulling to break my water bag. I screamed! I called for my mother to come and help me. The doctor said, "Push and shut up. She was so unkind the way she spoke to me." "Push and shut up. Your mother didn't get you pregnant." After I gave a push it wasn't long before I heard my baby cry. I gave birth at 4:33 a.m. I was so glad it was over. I couldn't get angry with the doctor because I was relieved that my baby was born and the pain was gone!

She said, "Ms. Gibbon you have a boy and you did a good job." The nurse took my baby to the nursery room while the doctor removed the after birth. She told me to get some rest because it would be several hours before breakfast.

Since the doctor didn't put me to sleep I was very alert but real sore. It was difficult to go to sleep. I tossed and turned for a little while before I went to sleep. When it was time for breakfast the nurse woke me up. I had a bowl of oatmeal, fruit cocktail, one boiled egg, a slice of toast, and a small carton of orange juice.

Big Richard Bernard came to pick the baby and me up from the hospital. But our baby had to stay at the hospital until he gained more weight. He was disappointed that the baby wasn't coming home with us. He was a premature baby weighing 4 lbs. 4 ounces.

On my next visit, the nurse said, she had good news for me. My baby had a good appetite and that he was gaining weight. The nurse asked, "Is this your first baby?" "No, I have a ten-year-old daughter and a twelve-year-old son." She asked, "How much did they weigh?" My first son weighed 4 lbs. 5 oz and my daughter weighed 5 lbs. 6 oz. Then she told me, that I'd had to carry my last baby on a pillow until he weighs 5lbs. The said you have a lot of years between the last two babies." So she said, since your baby is a premature we need to keep him in an incubator.

I went to visit baby every day, so I could hold him and feed him. When I went there on Sunday, the Nurse said, "I have good news for you." Tomorrow your baby can go home with you." When I went back to the hospital on Monday, the doctor checked my baby again. He had gained enough weight and was ready to go home with me. The doctor gave me instructions on how to take care of him."

The doctor said my baby had gained enough weight. We were so happy I could take him home a week earlier.

My daughter asked, why do you have to carry the baby on a pillow? Then she asked, "Mama Can I stay home from school tomorrow?" No, Patricia, you can help me take care of him on the weekends. She was eager to help take care of her baby brother. She held her hands out about nine inches apart and said, "Is the baby this small?" "No." She moved her hands further apart and said, "Is he this big?" After we finished dinner I washed the dishes while she did her homework. My daughter had matured since her brother was at home. Monday morning, it was time for my six-week-old baby to come home. Big Richard took the day off from work to drive me to the hospital. We were excited to bring him home. I had to carry him on a pillow until he gained 5 pounds. I had to feed him a small amount of formula every two hours instead of every 4 hours. As we were getting ready to leave the hospital, the Nurse placed him on a pillow and demonstrated how I should handle him.

He wore his blue and white baby clothes with a little matching knit cap looking cute. He brought so much joy into our lives. Patricia enjoyed helping with her little brother. We gave him so much love before we knew it he was growing fast. When he grew large enough to play with her, she'd make him laugh. Every day she'd come home from school and get her homework done so, she could play with him.

It was 1968, a spring day, Patricia decided to teach her little brother how to walk. She stood his back against the wall in the living room. I was sitting nearby on the sofa. I watched her to see if she knew what she was going to do. After she stood him against the wall she moved a few inches away from him, then she clapped her hands calling him to come to her. He would take one step at a time, when she called him. She'd move a little farther away each time and continued to call him.

My daughter was only 11 years old, she figured out how to teach him to walk at eight months. My daughter taught me that children know and understand more than parent gives them credit. Children can teach adults a thing or two. when we listen. Patricia was always quiet; she didn't talk much until her little brother was born. She could play by herself all day quietly for hours! She was so quiet, sometimes I had to go look for her when it was meal time.

On the weekends Mr. Bernard would play his guitar. He knew I liked to sing so he taught me a song "My Mother's Eyes."

I finally got the idea of what he meant about putting feeling into the song. When I thought about my childhood how my parents taught me wrong from right. As he played the guitar I sang it. He said, "Yeah! Now you've got."

Then one day he taught me how to play that song on the piano! I was so excited to play the piano and sing the song! I am grateful for the valuable things I learned from him

It's a good thing he didn't want to marry because he was 30 years older than me. I moved on with my life! I got a job, and my own apartment.

Chapter 21

MET MY FUTURE HUSBAND, 1969

One afternoon, I went shopping for some shoes at Sears and Roebuck. While shopping, I went to the employment department to see if they were hiring. Yes, they were hiring. I started working the next week. Every day I went to work I'd stop by the grocery store to buy a sandwich for lunch. Every time I went to the store, the manager would stop whatever he was doing so he could check me out at the register.

After the third week of shopping I didn't see the manager in his booth. I thought it was his day off. So I was going to grab some lunch items in a hurry and leave. I had an idea he liked me but I wasn't ready to date. After my first husband forced me to drink a fifth of whiskey by holding a gun on me, it caused me to be leery of men.

It was just a thought because it had not been long since I was divorced. I walked to the deli aisle looking for the lunch items. To my surprise I bumped right into him. Our backs were turned to each other. He was doing the inventory of the things that he was out of. I was walking backward, and I bumped into him accidently. Oops! I'm sorry. He smiled and said, "That was a nice bump, let's try that again." I blushed and began to walk away. I was wearing a Kelly-green dress with the zipper in the back, and Kelly-green shoes. "You're looking nice today as usual." Thank you I said, and kept walking. After I passed by him a few steps, he said wait.

"Young lady your dress is unzipped, do you mind if I zip it up." With head tilted down and my hand covering my eyes, I stood still and blushed. For some reason I thought, now that he already seen my dress unzipped I might as well let him zip it up. He let me know he was there to help by saying I just want you to look your best. After that it didn't take me long to get over my embarrassment. "Now that you let me zip it up, "Do I get to know your name and get a phone number?" I blushed. I gave him a smile and with a sigh, I said okay, my name is Kamiah.

He said, "I like your name Kamiah, it's beautiful just like you." I was glad I met Jeremy because he was very mature, and he had plans to have me in his future. On the other hand, Big Richard didn't have a future planned with me.

When I met Jeremy, he made it known to me that he had plans to start his own business. He inspired me with a presentation of how to own my own business as well. But I took my time to get to know him. I continued going to work at Sears. Every day I'd stop by the grocery store to say hello to him.

I had been living with Mr. Bernard for seven years, I knew I wanted more out of life than a common-law marriage. When I met Jeremy, I knew from my past relationship, I had to take it slow on dating again. Since I was so young when I first married I took my time to make a major decision, and dating was one of them! That's why I didn't rush into another relationship. It wasn't a smart thing to do.

I didn't leave Big Richard right away. I worked part time as a waitress at a Chinese Restaurant. I was happy to be earning my own money. Since I was uncertain about where I wanted to go. I asked him to buy me a piano while I stayed with him a little longer. It had been years since I had my first piano lesson from my mother.

I also wanted to play songs with him when he played his guitar. He liked the idea. He bought me a used piano for $200.00; it was in good shape. It gave me an incentive to take a music class.

I signed up for two semesters. When I first moved in with him I shared with him my interest in playing a piano. So Big Richard bought me the piano, then I started my music education. After I learned how to play a few songs on the piano, he would play along with me on his guitar.

He bought me whatever I wanted, but the only problem was he wouldn't marry me. He told me that he didn't want to put his thumb under the hammer ever again. That made it clear to me that he'd never marry again. It helped me realize that I could date other people.

Now that I'm older and reflect over my life today, I believe those years that I lived with Big Richard were no mistake. It was a time for me to heal from the abuse that I went through in my first marriage.

When I got to know Jeremy better, it helped me to decide that the timing was right to leave big Richard. Before I got serious about dating Jeremy, I let him know that I had three children. I let him know that my children and I come as a package. They go where I go. I needed to know in case he didn't want to be a family man. I wanted to be honest with him up front. I knew it was the right thing to do just in case he decided to marry me.

Since I met Jeremy on his job that was a plus for me. I got a chance to know where he worked. He was the store manager at the grocery store. I didn't have to ask him what kind of work he did because I knew. He was always polite to me whenever I stopped by the store. Every day I'd stop by the store to purchase a few items for my lunch before I went to work.

One day I purchased several items which filled up one large grocery bag and he said, "Let me take this to your car for you." "No thanks, it's not heavy." I knew he was flirting with me but I was shy. I really didn't think I was ready to be dating at that time. My abusive relationship with my x-husband had me afraid to date other men at that time. I was looking forward to getting my own apartment and stay away from relationships for a while.

When I met Jeremy, I was 29 years old, it was so different from when I ran away from home when I met my first husband Harold at age fourteen. First, Jeremy was at his place of employment so I didn't have to guess where he worked. I even had the privilege of knowing that his status was the store manager. The more I went there to shop; he began to show me attention. He made it known that he wanted to get to know me.

While he was calculating my items at the cash register I took the opportunity to check him out. Get it. Check him out. I didn't want him to know it, at least not right away that I was attracted to him too.

One day, when I stopped at the market where Jeremy worked, it was the first time I saw how handsome he really was. He was wearing a dark brown business suit. He had a neatly trimmed black mustache. I saw that there was something unique about him. When our eyes met, I noticed we both had light brown eyes. I saw a twinkle in his eyes as he looked at me. Or was it that, I was willing to take a chance to be in a relationship again.

I liked the way he said, I'd like to get to know you. My response was that I would stop back by his store from time to time. At this point, Jeremy and I had been seeing each other for two months. I let him know that I was living with an older man because I don't believe in dating two people at the same time.

Then I explained to Jeremy that I was renting a room from Big Richard, we were not in a serious relationship. I just didn't have nowhere else to live. I had been living with Big Richard for a few years. I lost my job working at a towel factory and was unable to pay my rent.

He said, he'd consider the rent paid if I'd sleep with him. I thought I'd have nothing to lose if I slept with him because I thought he was too old to get me pregnant. I found out that I was thinking wrong because I ended up pregnant. My baby was 2 ½ years old at the time I explained the situation to Jeremy that I had made a mistake.

My sister Rhonda was babysitting for me when I went to lunch with Jeremy. He was on his lunch hour. We rode in his blue Malibu Chevrolet left my red Chevy Corvette parked at the store, then we went to the Seafood Café. It didn't take us long to drive to the Seafood Café. The café was a small round building made with serving windows all around it. When the customers drove up, therefore waiters came to our car to call in our order over the intercom. We stayed in the car and the waiter brought our food to us. It was a beautiful day, so, we chose to sit at the tables covered with umbrellas in an outdoor patio. We had to chase the pesky birds away. We ended up getting back in the car to enjoy our lunch. We had fried shrimp with a spicy shrimp cocktail sauce, fried red snapper with crinkled cut crispy French fries. The side dishes were cold slaw with a sweet tangy salad dressing. We had a choice of green beans or collard greens cooked and seasoned with smoked ham hocks. When I ate the Jalapeño cornbread hush puppies, it was the best I ever had. I had to buy some to take home with me! On the menu was jalapeño cornbread hush puppies, crisp and fluffy. Also, a thirst quenching ice cold strawberry soda pop. Yummy! The Seafood really hit the spot. It was delicious!

After we returned to market, he asked, "When can I see you again?" I'll stop by Monday, on my way to work. After we pulled up in the parking lot he gave me his telephone number. I noticed the area code was a long-distance call for me. I let him know I couldn't call him because it would show up on my phone bill and I'd get in trouble.

Then, he gave me his job telephone number. So I could call him. "Now you don't have an excuse because the market's telephone number is in your area code." I agreed with him and gave him a call. He thanked me for calling and he told me to get well soon.

Chapter 21a - Working At Sears

I called my supervisor, Monday morning to let her know I was too ill to come to work. I worked at Sears and Roebuck's Catalog Department for five months. A week later, I notified her that I had to resign because the job was too hard for me. I thanked her for the opportunity of working there. She said she'd have my pay check ready on Friday.

I called Jeremy at the market. He asked if I was going to stop by to see him. I explained that I was ill and wouldn't see him until I was well. "I hope you get better real soon." "As soon as I'm better I'll stop by to see you." I thought I'd be over the flu in three days, but it lasted three weeks. I didn't call him until after a month

Jeremy called me to go to a business seminar with him. It was to learn how to own my own business. He was excited to tell me how I could earn a lot of money. At first, I was reluctant to go, but when he explained how it would be my own cosmetic business to earn a lot of money. I agreed to go to the meeting. I told Big Richard that I was going to into my own business. I also said I have a seminar to attend on Tuesday. He said, "Having your own business sounded great."

Jeremy came to my house on Tuesday evening. He gave me a ride to the seminar. We stayed out longer than I expected. It was 2:00 a.m. when I got home. Big Richard got home before I did. I went into the house all excited to show him my Holiday Magic kit. But he was upset because I came home late. He told me he didn't like me staying out after eleven O'clock at night.

He said, "if you have anywhere to go make sure do it while I'm at work." When I came home after 2:00 in the morning, he was furious! He waited until I got in bed and asked, "Why did you come home so late?" I yelled! Wait a minute. I came home as soon as the meeting was over. He raised his voice in anger. He grabbed the Pepsi Cola bottle off the nightstand. He held me down by sitting on my stomach. He shook the bottle in my face threatening me. "You'll never go out with another man again as long as I..." Before he got the words out of his mouth, I had reversed the situation instantly.!

In anger, I flipped him off me. I was on top of him shaking the bottle in his face. I pinned him down on his back by sitting on his stomach. I was gritting my teeth while saying, "You can't tell me what to do. I'm not your wife. He was shocked.

The amount of strength I had, it shocked me too. I knew it was supernatural strength that I had. I only weighed 120 pounds and was 5 feet 2 inches tall. He was 6 feet tall and weighed about 175 pounds. He had a slender physique. I am a person who doesn't like to fight. But when he threatened me and had me pinned on my back, I felt a surge of energy come into my body. It helped me to defend myself! I shook the bottle in his face. From that day on, he gave me respect. Just because I was 5 feet 2, didn't mean I was a weakling. He didn't know who he was messing with. He never again questioned me about where I was going or where I had been.

I know it was no accident that I had enough strength to keep him from hitting me. God gave me the strength to defend myself. After I reversed the situation, I just wanted to scare the "hell" out of him. I had lived with him for seven years. Little Richard was 2 years old. I realized there was no future with him. So I needed to move on with my life.

After Big Richard left for work, I called Jeremy. I let him know I was ready to move.

We drove across town to find an apartment for me to rent. We found a furnished apartment that was just what I needed.

Jeremy drove his car into the driveway right in front of the door. We loaded the car with my possessions. We drove off in a hurry to my new apartment.

I only lived there for three months, then Jeremy found another apartment for me that was close to where he lived. We went out once a week. Our first date was at the bowling alley. It was my first time bowling, I tripped and fell. He extended his hand to help me stand. He said, "Concentrate on where you want the ball to go. Focus on the center arrow, then aim to hit the center pin. After he gave me a little pep talk, I threw the ball. It knocked all the bowling pins down with one hit. Guess what?

When he took a few steps forward to release the ball it rolled straight, then it rolled down the gutter. He missed all the pins. He tried to brush it off by saying he accidently twisted his hand. It was so funny to me but I didn't laugh at him. I kept my chuckle to myself because he didn't laugh at me when I fell.

I took my time to aim the ball to where I wanted it to go. I struck all the pins down again. This time, instead of hugging me, he placed his hand on my shoulder and said, "I bet you can't do that again."

I took him up on his bet. I picked up the bowling ball with confidence. I threw the ball, then walked away. I heard the bowling pins fall. When I turned around to look, it was another strike.

When I made two strikes in a roll, he looked baffled. He said "Ah! That was just beginners luck. I looked at him as he sat at the scoring table. To make him feel better, I gave him a compliment about losing the game. I said, Jeremy that wasn't luck for me it happened because you're an excellent teacher. After I told him that he straightened up his shoulders and stuck his chest out with a big smile on his face.

Chapter 21b - Dating Jeremy, 1969

Even if I didn't make two strikes in a roll while bowling, I would've been just as happy as having a good time with him. After, he said that my second strike was by beginner's luck, it made me think he doubted my ability to learn. I suggested that we play at least two more games before we quit. I wanted him to win another game so we could break even.

By the time the bowling game ended we broke even. While walking toward the car he asked me if I'd like to meet his friends before going home. I agreed to go with him. We drove to Alta Dena, which was about a thirty-minute drive one way from Compton. He rang the doorbell. A distinguished man answered the door. He welcomed us in with a hug. After meeting Carl and his wife Martha, we walked through a hallway to the living room where Martha stopped to talk with me. She had the most beautiful smile. We have so much fun with the couple, I forgot about being shy. I was glad I met them.

Once I received her approval I was at ease. She offered us vodka with orange juice. After I had a few sips of the drink I felt relaxed. I joined their conversation. Carl asked us, if we would like to play a few domino games. We said we'd have to make a rain check on the game since it was late

I lost my job, and couldn't afford the apartment any longer. Jeremy asked me if I wanted to live with him. I didn't hesitate to accept! I didn't know any other place to move. I called Josephine a friend of the family to keep my two children until I found a place large enough for us. My oldest son Michael was 15 when he came to live with me. He had been living with his grandmother ever since he was 7 months old.

Chapter 21c - Prayed For Furniture

I worked for a year to save up enough money to rent an apartment. I didn't have money to buy furniture so I lived with Jeremy until I could buy some. We went to a new and used furniture store. But after I checked the price tags on the furniture, I only had enough money to buy one item. Jeremy and I sat in the car wondering where we could find a store with lower prices.

At that moment, I thought about a prayer my sister Rhonda told me to pray. She said, "When we pray with faith, believe that we have already received what it is we prayed for. She gave me this Scripture: Mark 11:24. And it says: "Therefore I say unto you, what things so ever ye desire when ye pray, believe that ye receive them, and ye shall have them." She said, "We need faith to believe we have something before we actually see it. We must believe by "faith" that we have it, and it shall come to pass if we only believe.

Jeremy and I were still sitting in the car when the store owner came running to talk to us. He waved his hand telling us to come back. Let's talk. We went back into the store to talk to him. "What do you need to buy?" I answered him, I need all the things to furnish a two-bedroom apartment.

The owner asked me, "How much money do you have?" I have $200.00. Then he said, "Don't look at the price tag, just select the items and we'll make a deal."

We walked through the store to select the things I needed. I chose a stove and a refrigerator for the kitchen. For the bedrooms, I selected a queen size bed, two bunk beds, and a single bed. The owner led us to the living room section; I chose a plush sofa, a recliner chair, and a dining room table set. I showed him my selections. He said, "How soon do you need these items?" "I need them today.

He said, "Okay hand me the $200.00, it's a deal." After I paid him, he said, "Young lady you need a coffee table and some lamp tables too. Those were the extra things he gave me to sweeten the deal. We shook hands and he asked, "What's your address?" I gave him my address, it was two blocks away. It didn't take long for the truck driver to deliver my furniture.

As we left the store I kept saying, "Thank you Jesus, and thank you Jeremy." "You're welcome." Wow! I was so happy. I knew that God answered my prayer! I told my sister that when she told me to pray, believe and that I would receive just thank God as though I had already received whatever I desired. It amazed me that it worked. When Rhonda first shared with me that if I need something. all I needed to do is to "pray, believe and thank God as though I had already received it." At that time; it had no meaning to me.

This is my prayer, I prayed, Lord, I need furniture so my children can come live with me. After I prayed that prayer, I believed that I would receive what I had prayer for. I pray in Jesus' name, Amen! It's a true story. GOD answered my prayer.

God blessed me to get my two children back. Jeremy would bring groceries to us every week. We dated for 3 years. Then Jeremy and I agreed to live together for one year so, we'd know how we'd get along as a family. My children were obeying my fiancé and me, they went to school and did their chores too. Then after a year Jeremy asked me to marry him. He let me wear his initial ring until he could buy my engagement ring.

In the spring of 1972, he and I had been living together for six months. I received a telephone call from my ex-husband's cousin. Her name is Della Mae. She gave me shocking news. My oldest son was living with his grandparents, and they had died and he had nowhere to live. All the family members were looking for me to take care of him. He was 16 then.

At this point in the story, I need to clarify the fact that my son was 7 months when he lived with his grandparents. The only reason he lived with them is because I was paralyzed and seven months pregnant. I couldn't take care of my baby. That's when my mother-in-law took him. She promised to keep him until I was better. When I was better she reneged. She died in an auto accident. His grandfather died from natural causes.

I explained the situation to Jeremy about him living with his grandparents and how it all ended. I thought he'd change his mind about our engagement. But to my surprise he didn't back out. Instead he gave me a lot of moral support. He stepped into our family and treated them as if he was their father. He said, we'll just have to go get him. I was so ecstatic that I had my son back once again. I just kept thanking ELOHIM every day as I cried with tears of joy. Yes! I had tears of joy! I kept saying repeatedly, "Thank you Lord, thank you!" I didn't tell my son why he wasn't living with me right away. Since Jeremy never had children of his own, he asked me to stop crying before I made myself ill. He didn't understand that I wasn't sad; I was overjoyed to have him back. So, I went to the bathroom to cry privately. That's when I bawled like a baby while I held a wet towel over my face.

My fiancé wanted to make sure it was over between me and my ex-husband, so, he took me and my three children to meet with him. He was waiting at his cousin's house, so we could meet. When my fiancé and I met my ex-husband at his cousin's house, both men shook hands. I was standing next to my fiancé, I was trying to get my ex-husband to look at me, but he didn't want to give me eye contact. It had been 10 years since the last time we were together. That was when my ex-husband tried to kill me. So that's why he was so shocked to see me. After he held the gun on me to drink a fifth of liquor, he thought I was dead. My fiancé waited in the living room while my ex-husband and I went to the bedroom to talk. That was our time to make sure that we didn't have any unresolved issues to handle!

While we were dating he'd spend time with my children on his off days. I worked 3 days during the week and on weekends. He'd buy groceries and teach them how to cook and clean the apartment. Some weekends he'd take them to the race track. He kept a close watch over them whenever I had to work. He made sure they had lunch money and clothes for school. He treated them like he was their father from when we got married.

Chapter 22a - 1971 Tough Love!

My oldest son had been missing days from school. So on my off day I went to his school to check him. Their teacher showed me his report cards. Later on, a friend of mine told me that he was ditching school and working at an auto repair shop. He was helping a man work on cars.

I talked with my fiancé about him ditching school. So we gave him two options. He could stay in school while we'd provided for him, or he could take care of himself and live on his own.

Michael had a habit of coming home with motor oil on his hands. He'd soil the furniture. The first time he did it, I woke him up and gave him a warning. I said, Michael before you sit on the furniture I need you to take a shower and change your clothes. At that time, I didn't discuss it with him about missing school, because I forgot to. He went to the auto repair shop, he soiled my clean sofa with oil again.

When I came home from work he was asleep on the sofa in oily clothes again. I was upset with him. I whipped him with the extension cord. He jumped up off the sofa so fast. He grabbed a baseball bat. It was behind the front door. He was getting ready to hit me. What was about to happen next shocked him and me too. My daughter ran to the kitchen. She grabbed a butcher knife. She said, "Put the bat down or I'll stab you." "Mother makes me mind her, so you've got to mind her too."

Since my son had live with his grandparents for 15 years, he wasn't used to obeying my rules. Since he didn't abide by my rules, I demanded him to get out. After a few months, I was worried about him. I wondered where he was living. I let him know that I loved him. I let him know I was providing for him, but he had to obey the rules of my house. He was 16 then. I let him know he needed to abide by my rules. I knew my rules were fair for him. But he didn't know me as his mother. I was 15 years old when he was born.

My fiancé bought clothes for my children while we were dating. They didn't want for anything because he helped me to provide for them. I thought my children were happy having him as their step-dad. For some reason, my daughter decided to run away from home. She left home for three months. First, I thought someone could've kidnapped her. But she gave me a telephone call. I was happy to know she was doing well. She asked, "Mother can I come back home?" She was 16 ½ years old at the time.

Deep down in my heart I wanted to tell her yes, but I had a flashback moment. At age 14, I ran away from home, the first man found me married me. I didn't know that marriage was a lot of work. I thought, married people had fun. I wanted my parents to provide for me again. I wanted to go back to school too.

I asked my mother could I go back home, but she said, "No!" My mother said, "You made your bed hard. Now lay in it." I thought my parents didn't love me anymore. I expected my husband to be home more than my ex-husband was. He worked in the day and gambled at night. I didn't like for him to come to home at 1:00 or 2:00 O'clock in the morning after gambling. My mother gave me tough love. I didn't get to go back home, but it made me grow up to become a woman. Therefore, I decided to give my daughter some tough love too. I repeated the exact words my mother told me, "You made your bed hard so lay in it."

My daughter found somewhere to stay. Jeremy asked, "Why did she leave home?" She ran away to be with her friends. I worried about her for 3 months. I decided to treat her like my mother did me. My mother gave me tough love. So I gave my daughter tough love too.

My teenagers wanted to do their own thing, they didn't obey me. So I let them see how hard life is by letting them live on their own. I found out that life wasn't easy for me when I left home too. God blessed me to make it through my teen years, even though, I bumped my head up against plenty of brick walls (metaphorically speaking). I learned that I had to obey somebody's rules in life. I knew it would work for my son and daughter too.

After they left home to live on their own, it was difficult for me to turn my back on them. I prayed that their angels would watch over them for me.

I had to remember that my parents let me experience life the hard way, it worked for me. As I reflect over my life, I'm glad I experienced tough love! I learned a lot about life! Number one, I learned that I had to obey somebody's rules. I also, learned to be grateful for when my parents provided shelter, food, and clothing for me. Now I know that one day, my children will recognize that tough love is not so bad after all. I always prayed for them. I had faith that God would take care of them like he did me. That's when I could focus on my future. I made it through life, even though I didn't know it was God who was with me all the time.

I found out that tough love doesn't hurt a child, when a parent does it for their own good. I gave my children tough love in return, they show me love. I thank God, I did. People I meet say, that they turned out to be very respectable adults too.

Now, I was 29 years old. I knew that Jeremy was the man for me. After we dated for four years, then he proposed to me. Then he let me wear his initial ring, until he could buy me my own ring.

It was May 1973, the Memorial Day weekend when my teenage daughter ran away from home. I didn't know why she left home. It had been several months since they left home. I was worried about her because she was sixteen; neither did she have a job.

Jeremy and I looked for a house to buy. He asked me, what would my dream house look like? I'd like a two-story home with a swimming pool. With a big smile on his face, he said, "then that's what we'll look for." That impressed me about him!. He knows how to take care of business. He made sure that we'd have a home before getting married. "What would you do with a large home like that?" I'd cook big dinners so we could entertain our guests. Wow Jeremy said, "That's the same thing I had in mind, you're okay with me." I was glad he wanted me to help him select our home! My youngest son age 4 was living with us. The three of us went house hunting. It was four homes in all that we had in mind to discuss. So out of the four homes we viewed he asked, "Which one did you like best." Since this was my first time ever making a huge decision, he left it up to me to make the final decision. He was happy with my decision. It was awesome. I took a few minutes to reflect on the homes we considered and said, "I really love the last home we looked at." "Okay, that's the one we'll buy."

It was one of the best things that happened to me after all that I had been through. I was unaware that it was God who was divinely orchestrating our lives in the first place. It was a week or two after we made our final decision on the home we went to the bank to sign the real estate documents.

This was my second marriage so I chose a light blue bridal gown. The bouquet was made of blue flowers with white baby breath flowers mixed with them too. There was a long gold ribbon beautifully tied around it. It matched the gold trim on the bridal gown.

His sister Joyce offered to take me shopping to find my bridal gown. I wanted to treat her to lunch after we finished shopping. She told me "No, the treat is on me today. We'll go shopping again, I'll take a rain check. Is it alright with you?" I agreed.

It was two weeks later, Jeremy and I went shopping for our wedding rings. All the rings were beautiful; it made it difficult to select just one. Shopping for hours was getting tiring, so we stopped for a lunch break. We finally found a pair of matching rings.

Since he spent so much money on our wedding, we agreed to have our reception in our new home. He had a big surprise waiting for me when we got home. The caterers had prepared the food. His friends had our home decorated for the reception. It was blue and white crate paper streamers. The decorations hung from the ceiling with blue and white crate paper wedding bells hanging on them. It was beautiful!

We had over two hundred guests at our reception. There were chairs placed all through the house for them to sit. We had T.V. trays for them to use to eat their food. There were guests in the family room, where they had a beautiful view of our swimming pool. And there were guest sitting around the swimming with T.V. trays to eat their dinner. The ivy plants covered a six-foot high fence that surrounded the backyard to give us privacy. We had red roses in vases, we placed them in the backyard and throughout the entire house. I went to my mother-in-law's beautician to get my hair done the day before my wedding. The beautician styled my hair with a French roll in the back. I had curls in the front combed to the left side of my face. My fingernails were a medium length and polished with a silver frost color. It matched my wedding gown.

Before we got married my fiancé and I lived apart for two weeks. We called each other every single day. Wow! That was the longest two weeks I ever had. It was hard for me to sleep, I woke up every hour.

Chapter 23

OUR WEDDING DAY

I had finished putting on my veil and gold high heel shoes when I heard the front door open. I knew it was my groom coming in because he was the only one with a key to my apartment. I was happy that I'd soon be with him; my heart was beating fast with excitement. I started walking fast from my bedroom to the living room; we had big smiles on our faces as we met and gave each other a big hug. He was looking handsome from head to toe, with his neatly trimmed haircut. He wore a black tuxedo with a powder blue shirt with small ruffles in the front; with a black bowtie, also black patent leather shoes.

We left the house headed for the church to get there on time. He drove us in the custom-made car he custom built while we were dating. The body of the car was like a Chevy Corvette. It was a two-door sports car covered with royal blue crushed velvet fabric. It was beautiful; everybody watched us as we drove on our way to the church. We arrived just in time to meet with the Pastor.

We gave him a monetary gift in advance; to carry out our wedding vows.

I waited in the woman's lounge until Sunday School was over. It was my wedding day! My fiancé was already at the church waiting for me to arrive.

Right after Sunday school, the organist played the wedding march song. That was the Pastor's cue to stand at the podium. He waited there for my fiancé to come from the men's lounge to join him. My fiancé looked so handsome from head to toe. He had a neatly trimmed mustache and haircut. He wore a black tuxedo with a powder blue shirt with small ruffles in the front with a black bowtie, and also black patent leather shoes. Next, his brother Norman joined him at the altar; he was his best man. He wore a black tuxedo with a white shirt and bowtie. My sister Rhonda was my maid of honor. She marched down the aisle wearing a beautiful soft pink evening gown. She had a matching pink flower hair peace that she wore on the crown of her head.

The organist started playing the wedding march song before I came out. I had my hair done the day before my wedding. The beautician styled my hair with a French roll in the back. I had curls in the front combed to the left side of my face. My fingernails were polished with a silver frost color they were a medium length. This was my second marriage, so, I wore powder blue for my wedding gown. My bridal gown had an A-line shape with 3-tier ruffles! The first tier was small that's just below the breast. The next tier was a medium length around the waist. The bottom tier of my dress was large, that flowed into a circle that touched the floor. There were metallic gold ribbons sewn to each tier of my wedding gown. The neckline was square with sleeve that tapered to a point at the wrist. The bridal bouquet was made with light blue flowers and white baby breath flowers with a gold ribbon bow tied around it. It matched the gold trim on the bridal gown.

Next, his brother Norman joined him at the altar.

My parents, my siblings, and my youngest son were there to witness our marriage also. We had so many guests at church there was standing room only.

The Pastor led us in prayer, then read our vows. He asked who gives this woman away. My father stood up and said I do. The Pastor said, "Jeremy will you take this woman to be your lawful wedded wife?" "I do." To love and cherish her until death do you part as God as your witness?" "I do." The Pastor speaking, "Kamiah do you take this man to be your lawful wedded husband?" To love and obey him, until death do you part as God as your witness?" "I do."

The Pastor said, "Jeremy, you may salute the bride." We embraced with a kiss. The reason we kissed so long we didn't see each other for two weeks prior to our wedding. That's what made it so special.

The Pastor pronounced us as Mr. and Mrs. Maury. We turned around to face the congregation as they applauded us with a standing ovation. It didn't take us long to get married. Our ceremony lasted 15 minutes; did we beat the world's Guinness book of records? Maybe we did beat . For the remainder of the service, we sat on the front row to join the congregation. He whispered in my ear to let me know that Ms. Perry paid for the food and refreshments for our reception. It was a surprise for me. When I wanted to hire a caterer, he told me not to worry about it. His brother went to open our home to let the caterers in to deliver the food. We stood on the front steps of the church while family and friends took pictures of us. When the service was over, my husband and I led the congregation to the outside of the church. We stood on the front steps of church. People were taking pictures of us. Family and friends threw rice over our head! We had to push through the crowd to get to our car. It was on the parking lot across the street.

When I purchased my wedding dress, I didn't know it was going to match the color of our blue car! He drove us in his custom-built car. He built it while we were dating. The body of the car was like a Chevy Corvette. It was a two-door sports car covered with royal blue crushed velvet fabric. I dated him while he was building the car. It was beautiful church members watched us as we drove away to go home. When we arrived at the house some of our guests were waiting for us. After we parked in the driveway, favorite Uncle came to greet us. He said, "You two look rich in your blue velvet car." He was affluent, for him to give us a compliment that we looked rich; he didn't receive it lightly.

Our photographer took so many pictures of us; I was tired of smiling. For our reception, the caterer prepared a variety of delicious foods. Our guest served themselves from the buffet table. There were so many people that some had to sit outside in the patio near the swimming pool. One thing we forgot was to limit the time for the reception to end. Some of the guest stayed way too long. We had smiled so long, we had smiles glued on our faces when we went to bed. When the last guest finally left we were too exhausted for romance.

The next morning, we went to a beach front restaurant for breakfast. We had crispy fried bacon and scrambled eggs with a side order of hot crispy waffles; served with melted butter, maple syrup, and coffee. It was delicious! After breakfast, we took an hour walk on the beach front; it was so romantic! It was on a beautiful autumn day; the sun was shining, and there was a chill in the air. We had on our warm coats. I was so happy to relax after the wedding was over.

It was 1974, we had been married for a year. One day, I was at home taking a break from working with my husband on the rental property. I was in my jogging clothes cooking and cleaning our home.

The doorbell rang, I rushed to answer it. A lady was standing there dressed in a light blue suit; the fragrance she wore was pleasant. I was impressed how nice she looked. With a big smile on her face, she said, Avon calling. Her smile was contagious and she was friendly. I invited her in so I could look through her sales book. I was having so much fun that I could order cosmetics in the comfort of my home. I was so impressed. I asked, how can I become an Avon Representative? She responded, "I can sign you up right now." Wow! I was so excited that I could earn my own income!

It was even better to work my own hours. That way I could pick up my son Richard from school plus have dinner ready. I worked for Avon 4 hours 3 days a week. I helped my husband refurbish our income property 2 days a week. It was convenient for me to schedule my own hours. I let my husband know I could still help him work on our income property! We had been married for a year. I worked for Avon 4 hours 3 days a week. I helped my husband refurbish our income property 2 days a week. It was convenient for me to schedule my own hours. I let my husband know I could still help work on the rental apartments!

Selling Avon Products was a fun job for me. I had fun dressing up going to work. My customers always knew what they wanted to buy. After selling Avon products for five years became a team leader.

Chapter 24

ECTOPIC PREGNANCY

My youngest son was 8 years old, then. So I thought it would be nice to have another child. Jeremy and I agreed that we'd had a child; this would be his first. I went to the doctor to have an "IUD birth control device" removed so I could get pregnant.

I disrobed to put on the light blue clinic gown. The nurse led me to the examination room. When I had the birth control device removed I was expecting to feel discomfort. But it didn't hurt me at all. I was so excited. That we'd be able to have a child.

It didn't take long for me to become pregnant. After I was 3 months pregnant, I had a miscarriage. I tried for the next five years to get pregnant, but I ended up with having three more miscarriages. By the time I became pregnant for the fourth time, it almost took me my life.

When I became pregnant for the fourth time, I stayed pregnant until my third trimester. On this day, I was going to collect the rent from one of our tenants! I drove to the apartments which was four blocks from where we lived. When I got there, I climbed a flight of stairs. I was happy that we were going to have a child. I greeted the tenant and she gave me her rental payment. We had a short conversation. When I went back down the stairway, I felt a severe pain in my left side. It hurt so badly I thought I was going to pass out. I grabbed my side. I was moaning and groaning, having the worst pain I ever had. I walked slowly down the stairway with tears in my eyes. I took my time walking to the car. But once I got into the car I drove fast, I was frightened. I didn't know what was happening to my body.

As soon as I got home, I bent over in severe pain. Holding my side as I moaned with every step. I walked slowly into my husband's office. He was talking on the telephone. I said to him as I moaned, "Honey, I need to go to the hospital." Whoever was on the other end of the telephone, he said to them, "I'll get back with you later okay?" He slammed the telephone down." He called little Richard to go with us, as he rushed me to the hospital.

Every bump we hit in the road caused my pain to intensify. I moaned with pain all the way to the hospital. The nurse rushed me into the triage room. The doctor said he didn't find any external bleeding in me; so he gave me medication for indigestion. Then he released me from the hospital. I was still in pain. The doctor told my husband to bring me back if I got worse.

After we got home I went to bed. I had so much pain it was difficult to sleep! Thank God, through the night I did get a little sleep every now and then. The next day was Monday, my husband took off from work to check on me. Since it was a holiday, little Richard was out of school that day also. My husband left our son at the house with me while he went across the street. He went to talk to his friend at the automotive repair shop.

It was about 2:00 in the afternoon, when I got out of bed to go to the restroom. I was feeling bloated and weak. While sitting on the toilet I was getting weaker. Thank God little Richard was close by when I called him. I was so weak I could only whisper. I called him, "Richard (I paused to breathe) Richard." He responded after I called him the second time. I heard him stop at the bathroom door.

I told him to bring me a pillow and a chair so I could lay my head down. When he returned with the chair and pillow, I didn't remember it. I had blacked out then I regained consciousness. That's when my husband was lifting me up off the toilet. He said, "I'm taking you to the hospital."

This time we went to a hospital that was closer to home. The name of the hospital was Rancho Dominguez Valley, it was a six-minute ride from our house. With every bump we hit in the road it intensified my pain. I heard the doctor tell a nurse to bring the largest syringe in the hospital. I had no idea what the largest syringe looked like. When the nurse brought back the syringe my eyes got so big they could've popped out of their sockets. I had to have emergency surgery.

The doctor called for four nurses to assist him. He had two nurses to hold my shoulders down. The other two nurses held my legs up and opened wide. The doctor said, "You're bleeding internally; I need to siphon the blood out of you." It was the biggest syringe I had ever seen in my life. Wow! It looked like the tube was about 3 feet long with a huge needle connected to it. The needle looked like it was 3 feet long. Oh my God! I was so terrified!

I knew one thing. Since the doctor commanded me not to move, I knew what I could do. I made up my mind that I could scream as loud as I wanted to. He didn't tape my shut. The doctor told me again with the tone of authority in his voice, "you better not move." After he said his last word, that's when I felt him push the gigantic syringe up through my vagina. It reached all the way into my chest area. I let out the loudest scream that I could. The people in the waiting area couldn't help but hear me scream. I screamed so loud. I have a very strong voice. I used all the strength I had to scream. After I finished screaming, I could barely speak above a whisper. My throat was sore.

After the doctor siphoned the blood out of me, he had to give me a transfusion. I had seven pints of blood. The nurses put 7 pints of blood by a syringe into the veins. I had needles going into my arms, wrist, legs, and ankles at one time. The doctor told the nurses rush me to the surgery room. The last thing I recall is when the anesthesiologist put a mask over my nose and mouth. He asked me to count backward from ten to number one.

I counted to the number seven then I was unconscious. (That was just 4 seconds that I counted. The next time I woke up, I found myself in the intensive care unit. I had tubes in my nose and a catheter inserted in me. A syringe was in my arm connected to an IV bottle. My husband and my parents came into the ICU to pray for me.

After surgery, I stayed in the ICU for three days. I had one of my lungs injured, when the doctor siphoned the blood out of me. I had severe pains in my chest when I coughed. The nurse that was with me in the recovery room tried to wake me but I didn't respond. She said she called me several times.

My first name is Kamiah, but my family members called me Nancy instead. The nurse called me to wake me up after surgery. I didn't respond.! She wondered why it took me so long to wake up.

It upset me when I found out my family changed my name from Kamiah to Nancy. They called me Nancy from when I was 2 months old up until I was in my forties. That's why I didn't recognize my real name Kamiah when the nurse called me. I could have died. When I didn't respond to the nurse's call. I didn't wake up right away after surgery because I wasn't used to my real name. I could've lost my life. When the nurse called me I didn't wake up right away.

I asked my mother, "Why did the family call me Nancy?" She said, "Your sister Rhonda named you after her classmate. She said you looked like her." I asked my sister, "Why did you change my name when I was two months old?" She said her friend at school was a beautiful girl. She liked her pretty name too. She said I was a beautiful baby too. That's why she named me after her friend. My sister Rhonda was only 8 ½ years old when I was born. She didn't know she did anything wrong. But my parents were the adults, I thought they would've known not to give me a nickname.

I read in a book that NAMES ARE EXPTREMELY IMPORTANT! Names connect us to our destiny in life. The name Nancy had me living a confused life. "The name Nancy means a flirtatious person." I was being flirtatious and didn't know it was because of that name!

I ask parents to find out what does your child's name mean. You may think twice before calling your children by nicknames. Their real name is special. It connects them to their destiny in life.

My name is Kamiah., it determines who I am and how I act. It also means that I'm a strong independent woman. I didn't find that out until I was in my fifties.

In the book of Genesis 17:5, it explains why God changed Abram's name to Abraham. "Abram means: "High Father." Abraham means: "Father of many nations."

Every time somebody called Abraham, they were calling him "Father of many nations." The name Abraham caused him to be the father of many nations. Our names define who we are. It determines our destination in life.

Because of that, I knew I had to tell my family members to stop calling me Nancy. The meaning of the name Nancy caused me to live my life as a flirtatious person. When I was a little girl nobody called me Kamiah. But that was my real name. So I didn't respond to it. The nurse said, she tried repeatedly, to wake me up after I had surgery. She said she was worried because I didn't respond to my real name. It confused me because my parents let one of my sibling's orally change my name. I'm so glad I convinced my relatives to call me by my birth name Kamiah.

It was so painful for me, when I found out my older sister was the one who verbally changed my name. My sister told me, I was 2 only months old when she did it. My sister convinced our parents to change my real name into the nickname, Nancy. She didn't know that names are our destiny in life. She was only 8 ½ years old. I learned from the Bible that God changed Abrams to Abraham, so that he would be the father of many nations. Names are very important, it shapes our character, and gives us our identity. I was being a promiscuous teenager because of the name Nancy. I'm still dealing with the pain from it. It's not as bad as it used to be. Now as I write my story at age 76, I know my mother didn't know the importance of a name! Otherwise, she wouldn't have let it happen! So, I forgave my mother for the name change! Parents don't know everything. I am a parent now, so, I understand parents can make mistakes too.

Chapter 24a - Hospital Visit From Son

The nurse let my son visit me in the hospital even though he was under age. When he walked into my room I was rubbing my face because it was hurting me. I spoke out loud, "I wonder why my face is hurting." He said, "Daddy slapped your face!" Why did he do that? "Mom your eyes were rolling around in your head! He was trying to wake you up!" The doctor said, "I had a 50/50 chance of living." He explained that he had to slap my face because my eyes were rolling around in my head. I was unconscious and blacked out. That's why he rushed me to the hospital. Wow! my husband must have hit me with all his might. My face was hurting so bad it felt like my jawbone was broken. All I can say is whatever it took to keep me alive. I thank God. My husband knew what to do to keep me alive. After surgery, the doctor told me that he had to remove my left fallopian tube. When the doctor told me that I didn't feel like a complete woman.

Since we were trying to have our first child, the doctor said I could still conceive with one fallopian tube. When I woke up from surgery I was in the recovery room. My lungs were hurting. I told the doctor. He said, I had internal bleeding and it infected my lungs. The doctor gave me antibiotics to clear up my infection. Thank God, I felt better in a week.

I needed to be home in time so my Avon customers could order gifts for Christmas; I was in the hospital longer than expected. I called my customers so they could place their orders from my hospital room. Avon processed their orders then sent them to my home. When I got home I called my customers, then they came to pick up their packages. To my surprise, God blessed me to receive one of my largest orders while I was in the hospital.

As I type this story God revealed to me that I used my faith without knowing it. When my parents and sister came to visit they helped me bag my customer's packages. They saw that I needed help and they pitched in.

I read the orders from the receipt book; my relatives filled the bag with each order for me. When I called the customers, they came to pick up their packages. That way I didn't have to exhaust myself so soon after surgery.

My customers thanked me that they got packages in time for Christmas. My relatives helped me at a time I needed it the most. I had Avon product boxes placed wall to wall in the living room. When I kept busy doing something I enjoyed, it made me realized I was getting stronger. I didn't focus on the pains. I'd lie down to take breaks between customers. After being home a couple of weeks, I got a surprise visit from my daughter. She said, "Mom I was at the hospital to visit you, but you were sleep. You were in the intensive care unit." I don't remember you coming. "Mom I know you didn't because you were sleep."

I noticed she had a baby in her arms when she came to my house. I hadn't seen her in two years. She handed me the baby on a pillow. I asked her, "Whose baby is this?" "This is your granddaughter." I was only thirty-five years old. I never imagined I'd be a grandmother that young. It didn't take me long to accept my first grandchild. I was proud of her. She's so beautiful with her curly black hair and little round face with slanted almond shaped eyes.

Now, I was 35 years old. It was in December 1975, when I nearly died. That was the worst pain I ever experienced. I was so close to death. At the same time when I held my first grandchild, it was so much joy, it offset the worst pain I ever had. It was one of my worse days and one of my best days at the same time.!

As I write this story, I look back over my life and see how God works everything for our good. Romans 8:28 says, "And we know that all things work together for good to them that love God, and are the called according to his purpose."

My daughter came back into my life at a time when we needed each other the most. I had just lost a baby through a painful ectopic pregnancy.

My daughter shared with me the severe pains she had while giving birth to her first child. I understood because I was still in pain when she came to visit me. I had compassion for her. She also understood my pain. By having my first grandbaby when I had just lost mine; it helped me not to be so sad.

After we shared our experience of motherhood, she said, "Mother, this is my first and last baby because that was too much pain." I said to her, my granddaughter needs a little brother or sister. "She has plenty of cousins to play with and that settles it." "Mother I'll never go through that horrible pain again." Just watch and see I really mean it. No more children for me." My daughter sure kept her word; she only had one child.

Chapter 25

A CARIBBEN CRUISE SHIP IN 1980

The doctor advised my husband and me that it would be healthy for me to get pregnant again. He told us about a surgery he could give me to keep my uterus closed. That way I wouldn't have a miscarriage. With only one fallopian tube, I didn't think if I could get pregnant. The doctor assured me that after the surgery I would stay pregnant.

The doctor reminded me to let him know as soon as I knew I was pregnant. That's when he would perform the surgery to close my uterus. It would keep me from having a miscarriage. It was good news for us because Jeremy was such a good father to my children.

We had a nice flight to Florida. It was my second time out of the United States. We had just enough time to catch a cab before boarding the Cruise ship. That evening there are no words for me to express how bad the pain felt from the ectopic pregnancy. It was so severe I'll never forget it. After all I had been through, my husband planned n a vacation for us to go on. The doctor liked the idea that my husband was taking me on a vacation. He said it would help me to relax mentally and physically.

Flying on an airplane wasn't my favorite thing to do. I had a martini to help me relax. I prayed too. The flight to Florida was six hours. I hung onto my husband's arm the entire trip. While we were getting off the airplane, I took a moment to thank God for a safe trip. A couple who were friends of ours asked us to go on a Caribbean Cruise with them. Since I had suffered from so much pain from the pregnancy, it was a great idea to have a relaxing vacation. The first trip my husband and I had was to Fairbanks, Alaska. Jeremy and I went for a walk on the deck. The Cruise Ship docked in Haiti. We toured the town for a day. Then we saw the town of Puerto Rico; I was having the time of my life.

After we returned home from our Caribbean Cruise, we went dirt bike riding. It was so much fun. I realized that it had been two months since I had my monthly cycle. I called my doctor; he gave me an exam. The test was positive; I was two months pregnant. It helped me to have a full-term pregnancy. Before the doctor gave me that special surgery I didn't think I could have another child.

The doctor gave me strict orders to stay in the bed for eight months. I could only get out of bed to go to the bathroom. I was eight months pregnant. The surgery was a success for me to have to have a full-term pregnancy. The doctor removed the sutures.

During my pregnancy, my husband hired my sister Johanna to take care of me. She'd cook delicious meals for us and cleaned the house. She asked me to make a list of all the chores and meals that I wanted each day. She said by having a list of everything that I needed done; she wouldn't have to disturb me. I liked her plan because it made it easier for me too.

It was January 1981, I was five months pregnant. I could feel my baby kicking. I was happy to share it with my sister. She'd say, ah! I'll be so glad when the baby is born. I'd tell her, "Oh yes! I'll be glad when the baby is born too." I thought about how I had 4 more months that I'd have to lie down. The larger my stomach got it was more difficult for me to sleep.

One day I was outside standing my front porch, my neighbor Earline said, "Girl I'm tired of looking at you pregnant. She lived directly across the street from me. She'd say, if you come out of the house one more time pregnant, I'm gonna knock you down so you can have that baby." Earline and her family were good friends of ours. I knew she was joking about knocking me down. I just laughed. I thought, if Earline is tired of seeing me pregnant how in the world does she think I feel. I was so tired. I just had to enjoy the journey of being pregnant. I knew it wasn't going to last forever.

For me to get my mind off how much time I had left, I'd practice playing the piano. I'd have fun writing my own songs and singing them.

I went to the doctor for my eighth month pregnancy check-up. He examined me with an ultra sound test. He said the baby and I were doing well. The baby was large enough not to fall out. He told me that I could go ride a bicycle if I wanted to. I laughed. I asked the doctor, "Are you serious?" Before he responded, he tapped me lightly on my knee and said to me, "No I'm just kidding." Wow! I thought to myself, I knew people would laugh at me riding a bicycle at eight months pregnant.

While I was at the doctor's office, he removed the stitches he used to close my uterus. It helped me to carry the baby full term. The doctor told me he didn't need to give me anything for pain; he explained it wouldn't hurt me.

I felt great after the doctor said that I didn't have to stay in bed any longer. Staying in bed for eight months was boring. But when I read my Bible. it gave me a piece of mind.

I could go shopping, wow! That was good news! My sister continued to work for me because the doctor didn't want me to push a vacuum cleaner or mop floors. Therefore, my sister was still taking care of the house for me; I would go to the mall. I enjoyed having lunch; then later I'd walked and window shop. I'd stop at Clifton's Restaurant to eat lunch. Yum! They had some delicious food.

My husband and I joined a Lamaze class. I learned the correct way to breathe during labor. When I went to bed that night, it was nine O'clock, and I lied down to rest. It was about an hour later I began feeling labor pains. I told my husband it was time for me to go to the hospital." We hurried to the car. I was moaning so loud; he pushed down on the accelerator pedal to go faster. We went to the Rancho Dominguez Valley hospital; it was only a few miles from our home.

I wanted to have a natural child birth, but I couldn't. The doctor had to rush me to the operation room. My water bag didn't break in time. I was on the delivery table, but I wasn't dilating properly. The doctor yelled at me. "Do you feel the pain yet?" I was doing my Lamaze breathing techniques. I answered the doctor by holding up one finger; I nodded my head yes.

The nurse prepared me for emergency surgery. The doctor gave me an epidural injection into my back. He said, "You better not move." "If you move it would be a chance you'd end up paralyzed. I made sure not to move.

After the injection became effective, I couldn't move my legs. I was wide awake when the doctor delivered my baby. I could hear him announcing with a proud voice, "It's a BOY." As soon as the nurse cleaned the baby up, she brought him around the other side of the partition where I could see him. I was still lying on the operating table and she let me hold him a few minutes.

The nurse was describing my baby to me. She said, "Oh, look at his sandy red hair and his light green eyes." The nurse was a young Caucasian with sandy red hair too. She said, "Please give him to me, everyone will think he's mine." If that nurse would've read my thoughts she would've known I didn't appreciate her asking for my baby. At first, I was getting upset. But I kept my thoughts to myself.

When I got to the maternity ward, my husband came to visit me. He wore a hospital gown over his clothing so he could hold our son. He leaned over and kissed my forehead and asked how was I feeling today? I responded, I can't move my legs. He sat near the bed to comfort me by holding my hand. My body was shaking because I had chills after the C-section. The doctor said, that it was normal to feel that way after surgery.

My husband called for the nurse to bring some warm blankets for me. She returned with the blanket and a surprise for me. She brought our baby boy for me to see. He was in his bassinette. He was born at 2:33 a.m.

Then I was 40. I was happy that I made the sacrifice for my husband to have his first child. He was a good father to my three children.

I know now that I'm older, I'd never want to go through another nine months of being bedridden again. Reading the Bible made the time pass faster for me. The reason for that is: I had happy thoughts to cheer me up every day.

When our baby boy was a few hours old, the nurse asked, "Do you have a name for him?" At that time, my husband wasn't ready to name our son. He told the nurse that he wanted to observe his personality first.

It made sense to me because our names are a very important part of our life.

On the second day after my surgery, I had a fever with a lot of pain. I was tired from the long hours of labor pains. I was glad that my husband took the responsibility to name our son. He wasn't satisfied with the names I had chosen. It was his first and only child; so I was happy for him to name his son.

It was early next morning, the nurse came to my room the day I was going home. She asked, "Did you and your husband agree on a name for your baby?" "I'll have to wait until he comes; he said he'd have a name for him today." When he came into my room, I told him the nurse was waiting for us to give her the name of our baby.

He smiled and said; "Our baby looks like a "Jason." How do you like that name?" Honey, that name is great. We gave each other a hug; when my husband finally named our baby.

Then I could go home. The nurse pushed me and the baby in a wheel chair to the car. It was a beautiful sunny day in the month of May.

When I got home from the hospital, she had a delicious dinner prepared for us. It made my mouth water. Yummy! After being in the hospital for five days, I was ready for some good home-cooked meals.

My other son Richard was fourteen. He went into the family room to see his baby brother. Baby Jason was in his bassinette asleep. He took one glance into the bassinette at his little brother without saying a word. I asked him, "What do you think of your little brother?" Richard smiled, he said, "He sure is tiny." I said to him, "When you were born, you were smaller than your little brother. You weighed 4lbs and 4 ounces, and Jason weighs 6 ½ lbs. Can you imagine that Richard?" He said, that's hard to believe that I was that small.

Our baby had been sleep most of the day. When my husband came home from work he was expecting relax after dinner. It had been 14 years since I had a baby, I forgot how it felt to have sleepless nights. We were ready to go to sleep.

We were in for a big shock. We were tired from a long day. That's when our baby was ready to wake up.

Shortly after we were in a deep sleep, we heard the baby crying. I wasn't fully awake trying to figure out now what do I do. I held my baby and rocked him. I changed his diaper. It didn't dawn on me he was hungry. So I began breast feeding him, and it was terribly painful.

The nurse told me that the more I nursed him my nipples should toughen up. For three months, I tried to nurse my baby; I kept waiting for the soreness to stop. But it didn't. One day I was nursing him, he was three months old at the time; he clamped his little gums down on my nipple real hard. With his gums still clamped tight on my nipple, he snatched his head straight back. Ouch! Then he snatched it to the side. Oh, my goodness it hurt.

That was the most painful experience I had while breast feeding one of my four children. I had to stop breast feeding him because my nipples were too sore. After that I fed him with a bottle. I tip my hat to all the mothers who breast feed their babies for a whole year, wow!

Since it had been fourteen years between Richard and little Jason, I had forgotten how to take care of a new born baby. Our baby was crying so much I called the nurses clinic to ask for instructions for what to do. In the emergency room, doctor examined our baby; he said there's nothing wrong with your baby.

He only has his nights and days mixed up. By not knowing how to care for our baby was the beginning of our marital problems. One morning after we woke up from a good night's sleep, we looked at each other and smiled. Simultaneously, we said "Wow! we slept all night." Jeremy said, "Baby let's go out for dinner tonight to celebrate."

One day I was playing peak a game with little Jason, he was eleven months old. I would stand him up on the side of the king size bed, then I would get down on my hands and knees at the end of the bed. I was hiding from him. I'd pat my hands on the floor and say "pap, pap, pap." Little Jason would hold on to the bed as he'd run toward me. I would put him back at the headboard. Every time we'd meet at the corner of the bed, I'd repeat the game over and over. The third time we met at the end of the bed, he kept running right past the bed. (LOL) That was when he learned how to run before he could walk. (LOL) He was running and laughing. It was so hilarious.

Before I realized it, time had passed by fast. Our baby was two years old. Just when I began to enjoy being a mother, Jeremy told me to put him in pre-school. I didn't like the idea of sending our baby to strangers so soon.

I wanted to stay home with him until he was at least five years old. Even though I didn't agree with my husband to enroll him in a pre-school, I did it to keep the peace.

Little Jason was just learning how to talk, so I didn't want to put him in a day care. Sure enough, 5 months after I enrolled him in the pre-school, a little girl bit him on the stomach. She left her teeth marks. I found out from a little boy who could talk good. He said a little girl bit him. She was the owner's granddaughter. I was upset with my husband for putting our son in a day care, before he could talk good.

After having our first child born, I realized that our views on how to raise a child was very different. It caused us to argue. We had marital problems because of that.

One of the disagreements was when Jeremy told me our son was too big for me to read him a bedtime story.

You don't need to be reading him stories. At the time, I didn't think too much about him telling me not to read to our son. Then one day I listened to a TV host say, how some parents can be jealous of their children. Why should a parent be jealous of their flesh? I don't understand it. But it happens. Children need both parents to love them

Chapter 26

BECAME A PIANO TEACHER

It seemed like the years went by fast for Jason to be graduating from kindergarten. Before I realized how much time had passed, he was in the third grade at a private school. I asked his teacher about his progress in class. She said he was looking around at others instead of doing his assignments. As soon as my son and I were in the car driving home, he said, "Mom, every time I raise my hand to get help from the teacher she ignores me. When I walk to her desk, she tells me to go and sit down.

The next day I asked the teacher about his behavior in class again. She put her hands on her hips and responded, "He doesn't pay attention when I give the class instructions. He disturbs the class by talking, when he should be working." Because of that, I offered to assist her in the classroom and she agreed to let me.

When my son needed help with his assignments, I made sure that he raised his hand and I waited for the teacher to respond. If I was in the classroom; it was obvious that the teacher recognized he raised his hand for help. I was also there to watch the teacher's interaction with the class too. I saw her giving favoritism to other students. Just like my son said she did. Of course, I knew she'd treat my son special because of my presence in the classroom.

One day, I was standing close to my son's teacher. She had the smell of liquor on her breath. Because I knew the teacher was drunk on the job I felt compelled to spend time at his school to check on all the children. I wanted to make sure she treated the entire class fair. They didn't have a musician for the choir. So I volunteered my time. I played the piano for them. Some days I would check with the principal to see if she needed assistance in her office. Sometimes we'd just sit and talk when she didn't have much work to do.

I was visiting the principal one day, she was sorting her mail. It was the first week in August 1990 during summer time. With excitement, she said to me, "Here's a letter for a piano teacher." I said, I'm a music teacher. She said "Ah! We need one. I thought, Oh! My God, I never taught music at a school. I heard a voice within me quietly saying, don't worry, have faith. The next words that came out of my mouth were how do I apply for the position? The principal answered, "You'll need to give the headmaster a letter regarding what you'll teach and the methods you use."

Bring it to the next school board meeting for approval. I shook her hand before I left and thanked her for the job. Before I started teaching at the school, I had a conversation with God as though I was talking to Him face to face. I said, God my Heavenly Father, "Okay LORD, I only know how to teach beginners music. Lord, I need your help." I heard from Him audibly say, "Teach what you know."

I continued talking with God as I drove home, I said, "Okay LORD I need your help. I'm stepping out in faith, and I'm trusting in you. I never taught group piano lessons in school." Again, I said, "LORD I need help with what to say in the letter.

I asked the LORD to show me where to find the books I needed for teaching. I said, "LORD I'm trusting in you with all my heart, and I thank you for my piano teaching job, in Jesus' name I pray Amen! I broke down crying with tears of joy. I knew it was God who ordered my steps in getting this job. I had no doubt in my mind. I could just see myself already teaching.

The reason why I felt so confident was, when I taught one student at a time my husband told me I needed to teach at a school. He knew I didn't have teaching credentials; he was trying to discourage me. He didn't like it because parents dropped off their children for their lessons.

My husband didn't know it; but he did me a favor when he stopped me from teaching at home. That favor was: God opened doors for me. He gave me a huge platform to teach piano lessons.

Instead of being discouraged by not teaching at home, I accepted it as a challenge.

Even though I didn't have credentials, I knew that I was capable to teach. I taught the students how to play the piano and sing at the same time. I give God the glory for that. I was grateful to be self-employed. I found so much joy to teach my students. When the children learned to play the piano so quickly, I knew it was because I asked God to help me teach them. God answered my prayers.

I asked God to help me find the right teaching materials. I went to the music book store; I didn't know beforehand what kind of music books I needed. After I went into the store, the first book shelf I came to I found the book I needed. It was God who guided me to find the teaching materials I needed. For me to qualify to be a piano instructor, I know that God opened the doors for me. From that point on, I knew I had to depend on God to help me teach my students. I do know that God works through people too. That's why I'm excited to share my story that God has done miraculous things in my life.

I called my younger sister, I shared the good news with her that I was teaching music at a school . With an attitude, she said, "How can you be a teacher? You don't have credentials." I answered, God qualified me with teaching credentials. He opened the doors for me too. Before I began teaching, I went to several schools to study music. Then I taught my students what I had learned.

My sister Doll and my husband were shocked when I told them I had a job teaching piano. When I had my first piano recital, I asked my husband to video tape it for me. I was shocked that he did it.

After I taught piano lessons for a year, one of the teachers enrolled her son in my class. Her son learned to play the piano and sing songs so quickly, she was shocked.

After the teacher's son was in my class for six months, she transferred to another school. She found out that the new school didn't have a music curriculum. So she called me to see if I wanted to teach at another school. Yes, I'd love to. She gave me the principal's telephone number. The principal and I met at a restaurant; I showed her my resume and the music lesson plan. I explained that I teach group lessons. She asked, "Well how much does the school need to pay for your services?" With a big smile I said, the parents pay me directly."

Mrs. Lambert told me, she was excited to have my music program at her school. She hired me the same day. She said, Mrs. Maury, I'd like for to come to the assembly meeting tomorrow night to tell the parents about your music class. I got so nervous. But after I prayed, God gave me courage. Then I was okay.

On parent and teacher's assembly night, I displayed my music books on a large table for them to see what I teach. With it I had a form for them. I was so happy to see how many parents signed up for my class that night. The parents came to the table to meet me. I began teaching my first-class, the next day. God opened the doors that I couldn't see. It was a miracle for me to teach at a school. I worked 2 hours a day for a total of 8 hours 4 days a week.

When I am afraid of doing something, this is the Scripture I quote, 2 Timothy 1:7. It says, "For God hath not given us the spirit of fear; but of power, and of love, and of a sound mind." I kept quoting that scripture until my fear ceased. I knew God gave me favor with my piano teaching business. I thank God for giving me the gift to teach.

At the end of the school year, I gave a piano recital. For my first one I had 80 students who performed. It was in the first week in June of 1991.

For my first piano recital at my church, my Pastor said, it would be okay for me to have it there. But the church was in a big mess on the day of the event. The dining room and kitchen was in a big mess too. We were shocked. We saw the sanctuary was in a mess too. The carpenters remodeled the church, the restrooms, and the Pastor's office, but they didn't clean up their mess.

Some of my friends and relatives arrived at the church early. They were all dressed up. When they saw the church in a mess, they said, "Kamiah don't worry about it." They all rolled up their sleeves, they had everything cleaned up and ready before my recital started.

I had so many things that I needed to do to get ready for the recital. When my relatives arrived they helped me put the decorations up in the church. I wanted my students to dress up for this occasion, it was their day to shine. It was a festive event for us.

My family and friends helped me to decorate the church. They hung black and white helium balloons in the ceiling. It was beautiful! We used crepe paper streamers to tie the balloons to. There were fifty to a hundred balloons on each crepe paper streamer. They alternated the colors with five black balloons, then five white until it covered the ribbons. In between the black and white balloons there were music notes. They hung the balloon streamers in the ceiling to create a large X. Balloon's hung from the ceiling in the dining room. They put fresh-cut red roses in vases to make center piece to decorate the dining room tables. Sitting the red roses in the middle of the black and white balloons, it looked so beautiful!

For the dining room table, they had multi-colored flowers in vases to place on each table. My sister in-law Jamie painted a basket white, she put black musical notes on it. She made it for my recital. It had live plants in it. I used it for the center piece to sit on the grand piano in the main sanctuary. The church was located at 89th, Compton Avenue in Los Angeles.

The Pastor left the church in a mess to discourage us. He meant it for evil but God turned into good for us God turned it into a miracle when my family and friends cleaned the church within one hour. Wow! I was relieved to know my friends and family members would go the extra mile to help me.

I had the cake decorated with music notes and a piano on it. I had expensive door prizes donated from two local stores. That way the guest could get a chance to win a door prized, they had to purchase tickets at the door.

The head master said, "Mrs. Maury, Did you get help paying for the dinners and the decorations?" I answered, no. I paid for everything. She said, "The parents would be happy to help you; all you need to do is ask for their help. "Don't try to do it all by yourself next time, okay?" The next time I had the piano recital, I wrote a list of things that I needed. I was so happy that I had help. The parent's, family members and friends paid for all the food and decorations.

The president of the advisory board at the school approved of my teaching skills! So, she enrolled two of her children into my class. Her two children were in pre-school at that time.

She told me how pleased she was with how fast her children learned to play the piano. She asked, "How would you like to teach at the community college for the "Kollege for Kids" program? I gladly accepted the position. I had no idea how big my music business would grow. My husband did me a favor when he didn't want me to teach at home. It worked out for my good. Praise God.

With God, there is nothing impossible. He blessed me when I accepted to teach at the first school. When I said, "LORD, I'm stepping out on faith! My music business came to be a reality! I trusted in the Lord with all my heart and lean not to my understanding. He guided me every step on how teach my students. I acknowledge the LORD in all me ways and he directed my path. That's when God opened the doors to 2 private schools and the college doors for me to teach piano lessons. (The scripture is Psalm 3:5, 6.)

Chapter 27

HUSBAND PLANS A TRIP WITHOUT ME

My husband tried to discourage me from teaching piano in many ways. Nothing he did worked. He made reservations to take a trip to Cancun, Mexico. I was shocked that he scheduled the trip on our 24th wedding anniversary. I thought he had planned a trip for us. But when he said, "If you want to go on the trip you can take whoever you want." I looked at him. I was shocked that he'd take a trip without me.

I was too angry to ask him who he was planning to take on the trip with him. He knew I didn't like flying on airplanes. He figured I'd let him go with whomever he wanted to take. But I shocked him. I told him we were going to take this trip. I told him, he wasn't taking this trip without me. Before that day, he had never seen me so assertive. We were sitting at the dining room table when I raised my voice and slammed my fist on the table. I really wanted to punch him in the face. I was so angry with him. I yelled, Jeremy, You're not taking this trip without me." He said, "Okay." All through our marriage he tried to get me to lose my cool. He finally found the right button to push.

I packed my sexy black bikini. My black negligee and I had white tight pant with a pastel tank top. When our airplane landed in Cancun Mexico, I treated him so nice it shocked him. He didn't know what to expect out of me. If we were in public place. I treated him like he was my friend!

Even though I didn't like flying on airplanes, I was so angry that I forgot about my fear of flying. I showed him that I demanded respect. Every time we were among the people I'd laugh and talk with him, instead of arguing. It was a beautiful place! So I enjoyed myself. I made it up in my mind to have fun with or without him.

After we arrived at the hotel, I thought about how it was going to be when we had to sleep together. When we went to bed that night, I made up my mind that I'd turn my back to him. I didn't want to sleep in his arms, I didn't want to kiss him either. I treated him as nice as I could without acting like I was his wife. I treated him more like a friend, instead of my lover.

I learned that day that my anger got rid of my fears. When I boarded the airplane, I was so excited to go on the trip. He thought, I would be too afraid to fly. No, I prayed and asked God to bless us to have a safe trip.

It was a miracle! For the first time in the history of me flying on airplanes, this time was the best flight I had. I didn't need an alcoholic beverage to calm my nerves like I did on other flights. I knew for a fact; for me to interrupt his plans, I had to trust God to take this flight. Then I knew I'd be safe.

I also asked God to remove all the anger that I had toward him. My husband had never seen my so verbal! We seldom had three words to say to each other all day when we were at home. Before we took the trip, he treated me like he wasn't in love with me anymore.

But I chose to have a good time while we were in Cancun, Mexico. As we walked in the downtown area, I enjoyed listening to the bands play Mexican music. We stopped to eat at a nice restaurant. We had refried beans with cheese burritos, wrapped in freshly warmed flour tortillas. We had peppers stuffed with melted cheese and corn chips. It was so delicious! Nobody had to tell me I was a queen that day, I felt like one. I was hoping that, that feeling would last forever.

For the first time in years, he was talking nice to me. But that was because we didn't talk about how we felt about each other. I enjoyed talking with him expressing our views on the beautiful scenery in the City of Cancun. One things I pointed out to him was, there were no billboard advertisements like we have in the United States. I didn't see none. The ocean water was warm and beautiful! The color was a sky blue, the sand was white on the beach front. The water was so clear we could see beautiful coral plants 5 feet below the ocean.

Instead of going out in the ocean on a sail boat, we walked on the sandy beach. We let our feet get wet in the warm ocean water. The waves began to rise high. The wind was blowing very strong. My hair was getting frizzy from the mist coming from the ocean air.

We returned to the hotel at 6:00, it was time for dinner. In the restaurant, we sat at a table with a beautiful ocean view. We watched the ocean while it was raging, the waves were crashing against the big rocks on the shoreline. The sun was beginning to set when he asked me would I like to walk on the beach to see the sunset.

Oh wow! I'd love to watch the sunset especially when the golden sun sits on the horizon of the ocean. The view was breathtaking. It's the most romantic thing I like to do with someone special. Since Jeremy and I were not on good terms, I had to enjoy the sunset without being romantic. After the sunset was gone, I thought, I could've put a spark back into our marriage by being romantic with him anyway. Who knows. Oh well, he looked like he had his mind made up about getting the divorce. While we were on the beach, I wanted to recapture our romantic moments so badly. But I refused to let him have the satisfaction of doing me wrong. I didn't want him to have the pleasure of thinking that I had forgiven him either.

Before he planned the trip he used to find fault with everything I did. I didn't realize it at the time that no matter how much I tried to do the right things, it was never good enough for him.

Chapter 28

JEREMY DIVORCED ME

He'd come home unexpectedly, to make his grand entrance. He slammed the front door against the wall. I didn't have to guess who was coming in. He stomped his feet in a hurry throughout the house. As though he'd catch me doing something wrong. He suspiciously looked in the closets and under the beds with an expression of dismay on his face. He searched the house. But didn't find me doing anything wrong.

He'd yell and say, "That's not the way to clean a house." I was cleaning the wall to wall mirrors in the family room which fit from the ceiling to the floor. I was cleaning them with a pink creamy cleansing product.

I felt on edge because he was yelling at me. I didn't like to argue with him, so I didn't say a word. I just stopped cleaning and sat down on the sofa. I gazed outside through the picture window. Looking at the water in the swimming pool relaxed me. I was trying to figure out why it was so difficult for me to please him. On top of that, I thought that if I'd do things his way it would keep down confusion. I thought, we'd get along better. WRONG! He began taking more trips out of town without me.

One day after he came home from a trip, I asked was he hungry? He said yes, but you don't need to cook because I'm taking you out to dinner. Surprisingly, I thought, well that's nice of him to take me out for dinner. But he's not looking very happy about it. I thought. He didn't have a smile on his face. However, I was glad that he took me out for dinner.

Our two sons were visiting relatives, it was just the two of us going out to dinner. He asked, "What restaurant would you like to go to?" I said, I'd like to go to the Red Lobster Restaurant in Lakewood." After we ordered our meal, he said the blessing and we began to eat. I ordered a lobster tail with melted butter, baked potato with butter, sour cream and chives, steamed broccoli, and Caesar salad with garlic and cheese biscuits. While I was eating, I must have taken about three bites of food, I noticed he wasn't eating.

He said "Kamiah, I need to tell you something." I stopped eating. I put the fork down waiting to hear the good news. Instead he said, "I want a divorce." Suddenly, I felt knots swelling up in my stomach. I lost my appetite. Tears rolled down my face. I broke down and cried. He called for the waitress to pack our food to go. When we finally went outside and got into our car I didn't say a word to him, I was so shocked.

It hurt me so bad. Words alone could not express the way I felt. He wanted a divorce. My body felt numb. It felt like he had just ripped my heart out of me. The thought of a divorce, it made me feel like death would be better.

After returning home, we went into the living room to look through our mail. We sat on the carpet in front of the fireplace. I thought about when we went to dinner, only for him to spoil it, by telling me he wanted a divorce.

At this point, I felt so bad, but I didn't want him to know it. I said, "I'm woman enough to accept that you don't want me. I expect you to be man enough to file for the divorce." I really didn't want a divorce, I was acting like I was tough and convinced myself that I'd be alright. My mother told me that if your spouse leaves you for someone else, you can't lose what you never had. She added if you really had them they would never leave. That is so true.

I looked at the fact, that I did everything a wife could do to please her husband. After he checked the mail, he walked out of the living room. He said, he'd see me later. I said, okay. When he left I, was hoping he'd come back. I wanted him to tell me he was joking about the divorce. He didn't come back until a week later. It felt like the weight of the world was on my shoulders. After I read the Bible and asked God to lead me, it made me feel so much better.

I was self-employed as a piano instructor. I worked part time as an Avon Representative. I prayed and read the Bible. I must have fallen asleep because the next thing I knew when I opened my eyes, the sun was shining through the drapes. It was morning and my Bible fell on the floor. Thank God, I did get some sleep.

He walked out on me. He took our son with him. So I went to the courthouse to file for a restraining order against him. He told me that I needed to move out of the house or he was going to move. After I came back home with my restraining order, I called a locksmith and had all the locks changed.

His excuse for divorcing me was he wanted to live on an island alone. I asked, him if we could get marriage counseling. It shocked me that he agreed for us to get counseling. After five sessions, the counselor counseled us one at a time. I asked him, "What can I do to keep my husband?" He said, there's nothing you can do by yourself to keep your marriage together. There's nothing wrong with you because your husband said, he loves you.

I accepted my husband's wish. I reminded, him to be man enough to get the get the divorce.

Next, he asked me to make a list of all the things that I want to keep out of the marriage. I wrote on my list: the five-piece sectional sofa, the refrigerator, and stove. I took the queen size bed and bedroom furniture. Then I listed one of the income properties and my Mercedes Benz.

Chapter 28 A - "Restraining Order"

I gathered up all the important documents I needed. Because of that I had a locksmith change all the locks on our home so I could search for all the documents on all the properties.

Just as I closed the large envelope with the documents, I heard knocking at the front door. He yelled! Open the door. I yelled back. Wait, just a minute. I hurried to the phone to call 911. In less than five minutes, there were four police officers outside talking to him, "Are you Jeremy M.?" He replied, yes Sir." Next the officer asked him, "Why do you need to get into the house?"

His response was, "I need to get my things out of there." The officer firmly said, "You only have five minutes to get whatever you need, and leave." The officer spoke loud enough for me to hear him through the door. He said, "Madam! Open the door. Jeremy is allowed five minutes to get whatever he needs." He didn't say a word to me because the four officers came into the house with him. They waited until he went into his office and got a few important documents together and he left.

Chapter 28b - "U-Haul Truck For Moving Me"

After he saw that the Officers came to protect me, he didn't come back to the house for a week. I'm sure he had someone watching to see when I left the house. One day, I went to work and when I returned home I was shocked. There was a U-Haul truck in front of my house. He had his friends to move all my possessions out of the house. I was shocked. I knew the man that was driving the U-Haul truck. I won't mention his name. He told me, that my husband sent him over to move me out of the house.

I had no idea where he was moving my things to. I was so devastated. I didn't think to ask questions. I couldn't figure out how they got into the house, after I had changed the locks. I was shocked. He put me out of my home. It was like a nightmare.

I asked him, "Where are you moving me to?" He said it's a block away. I didn't think could've called the police! They would've stopped him from moving me out of the house. I had a restraining order against him.

The driver handed me the keys to the house, after they finished moving me. It shocked me to see how small the house was because I was living in a two-story home.

Chapter 28c - Hired An Attorney

I hired an attorney that I found in the yellow pages. She was three blocks away from where I lived. Jeremy called and asked if I had an attorney? Yes, I answered. We met at my attorney's office. He asked her if she would mind settling our divorce in her office. She asked if I'd agree. My reply was yes. Prior to meeting with my attorney. He asked me to make a list of the things that I wanted before we separated.

I told my attorney how he had his friends pack my possessions and moved me. I didn't get a chance to see if they brought all my personal things. He wanted to keep all the income properties to himself that we owned together. But I worked too hard helping him refurbish the properties for him to keep it all.

The attorney made sure I got an equal share of the property. She convinced him to give me a 3-bedroom home and two six-unit apartment buildings. He bought me a Mercedes for my 50th birthday. When we divorced he wanted it back. The attorney read the list of things we agreed to divide up. He had a 25-foot motor home, a pick-up truck, and a two seat Mercedes that he kept for himself.

He hired an attorney too. I was so glad that I hired an attorney because he didn't have any intentions of being fair. My attorney made sure I received what was lawfully mine. The apartment units that he did agree to let me have were in bad shape.

The rental property I acquired was a challenge to take care of; but I was willing to take it on. It was therapy for me! I enjoyed being a property manager because I stayed busy. I didn't have time to be sad. I stepped out on faith to accept more challenges. I realized challenges helped me to learn new things. I learned how to deal with contractors. I wouldn't accept the first estimate, I'd always get two or three.

It was a challenge for me to take on all the responsibilities at one time. Not only did I have to collect rent, but I had to do credit checks, fix stopped up toilets, and patch holes in vacant apartments too. I took one day at a time. I focused on doing one task at a time. That's how I had to get the job done. Of course, I prayed for strength, and that kept me focused. Just don't give up.

I meditated on the word of God; then I confessed it over my circumstances. When I pray, God always shows me whatever it is that I need to do. Whenever I needed a repairman he'd lead me to the right one. This was time to strengthen my faith in God. Philippians 4:13, it says, "I can do all things through Christ which strengthens me." I literally trusted in the LORD with all my heart. I prayed before I did anything, and I'd ask Him to direct my path in everything. He always comes through for us!

Now back to when I owned and managed the 12 apartment units. For my secretarial duties, I had to screen potential tenants, evict non-paying tenants, and receive the rent payments. I had another tenant who stopped paying rent. She'd say she lost her job. She'd get two and three months behind. I served her with an eviction notice to only find out when she contested the court order, I couldn't collect rent. She could stay six months longer rent free. She left the apartment in a mess when she moved. I had to repair holes in the walls. I had to remove graffiti in every room. Plus, she stopped up the toilet. I thank God, I had the experience of being a landlady. It was a good feeling to learn new things!

Chapter 29

HIGH SPEED CHASE

One night at 11:00 p.m., the phone was ringing, it had startled me out of my sleep! One of my tenants called me about gang bangers selling drugs on the premises. I dressed myself in a hurry, I woke up my son Richard. We drove to the apartments less than five minutes!

When we arrived, there were so many vehicles parked in the driveway. I was shocked. I started to get out of my car, but I saw a guy sitting in his Jeep. He started it up, and drove toward me trying to hit my car. My son said in a quiet voice, "Mom, Mom, don't get out of the car. (My son has a gentle, but firm voice.) This looks like trouble! Let's go straight to the police station and report it." It's good to have sons! Especially, to help when things are out of control. It's just good to have 3 sons because they are a blessing. My one daughter is a blessing to me too!

I backed out of the driveway as fast as I could. As soon as I straightened up the car in the middle of the street, I drove forward and pressed down on the accelerator pedal. I drove as fast as I could. My son said I was driving 80 mph through the residential streets!

Every time I turned a corner we could hear the tires squeal! When I turned the corners in the car it slightly tilted to one side too. Richard said, "Mom hurry up." The guy is turning every corner we turn, hurry up!

I didn't have time to look in the rear-view mirror. I had to focus on the streets because people were still out walking. There was still traffic I had to avoid. The drug dealer was pursuing me at high speed as we weaved in and out of traffic. Finally, we drove up in the front of the Compton Sheriff Department. My son said, "The guy stopped chasing us. "Mom, do you know you were driving 80 mph on the residential streets?" I responded

"No!" This was the first time I was involved in a high-speed chase. I thank God that my son was with me. I thank God that I didn't get a ticket!

It was time for me to sell the income property. It was too many problems for me to handle. I had enough of being a landlady, so I sold the apartments. I didn't get enough money out of it, but I was glad to get rid of the headache!

Chapter 30 – Testimonies

GOD ORDERED MY STEPS

After the summer sessions at the College had ended, I was without a job.I had to work part-time at the private schools while waiting to return to the college.

While I was waiting for the college to return from their summer vacation, I still needed work to earn an income to pay my bills. So I went job searching.

The Los Angeles Unified School District was the first place I went to apply for a job. It was located at 79th Street and Vermont. The clerk gave me a typing test. I was looking for a clerical job. I waited a few minutes in the waiting room. I saw a lady who looked familiar to me. She had the most beautiful smile.! She called several people on the list ahead of me.

I said, "Excuse me for looking so hard at you, but you look like a person I used to know." She said, "You look familiar to me too." I asked, "Is Carl your husband?" She answered, "I used to be his wife. We're divorced and I remarried." She asked, "Is your name Kamiah, and Jeremy is your husband?" I responded, "Yes I am. However, Jeremy and I are divorced too." After that we gave each other a big hug. We had been friends for several years and had lost contact with each other.

God let me know it was no mistake that I found my friend Margie again! After I took my typing test even though I didn't pass it, it was still a blessing. She invited me to visit her church; I accepted. Since she knew I was a musician, she asked me would I like to sing at her brother's church where he is the Pastor.

She had a pleasant personality, and it was hard for me to say no to her. It was an honor for me to sing and play the piano at her brother's church. I love to give God the glory in everything I do. When she introduced me, the Pastor and church members gave me a warm welcome. I went to sit at the piano. I played my favorite song, "I Know Who Holds Tomorrow." That's my testimony song.

Since Margie and I met in 1969, we've been friends for over 40 years. We met while I was dating Jeremy. Before we became Christians, we used to drink liquor and have parties. It was a pleasant surprise, that after all those years, we both became born again believers.

She told me that she and her new husband Walter R had become ordained Pastors of the Gospel. So she asked me to visit their church. The first day I went to her church, I became a member.

They didn't have a musician, so they asked me to be their musician. I was happy to play the piano for them. The members voted me to be the church musician the first day I was there. I thought it over, then I joined their church on the first Sunday in October 2001. I enjoyed being a member of their church. It was small, but it was fill with the Holy Spirit. It's a blessing for us to be friends for life.

Chapter 30a Testimony -
A Gunman Randomly Shooting Cars

Three months had past. It was New Year's Day 2002, the first thing I did was praise God for blessing me to see another year. Later that day, I prepared music lessons for my students because school was about to begin in few days.

I work at Compton Community College then, but I had finished teaching my class. On March 12th of 2002, I took off from work as my son needed me to pick up my granddaughter from her school for him. I drove her to her aunt's house that lives in Los Angeles. I proceeded to do some shopping at a wig shop that was not too far away.

I travelled eastbound on the 10-freeway headed for home. But I changed my mind. I went to a wig boutique instead. I heard the voice of the LORD tell me to stay on the freeway and go home. I was just a few blocks away from the store on 59th street and Vermont Boulevard in Los Angeles. I ignored the voice of the LORD. I continued to the wig shop with my plans.

I exited the freeway on the Vermont off ramp going southbound. I was shocked, when I saw people driving in an erratic manner, They were crossing the double line facing the oncoming traffic. They were almost colliding with the other cars. The cars that were near the sidewalk sped sporadically going into the center lane. I was shocked. I yelled out loud. What on earth is wrong with these crazy drivers! I was in shock when I looked over my right shoulder, I saw a man standing on the sidewalk with a gun. He was aiming the gun right at me!

The people were driving bumper to bumper. They were desperately honking their horns. I was looking for a way to get out of congested traffic. When I found a way out, I jerked my steering wheel as fast as I could to get into the lane facing the oncoming traffic. A woman was driving facing me, going northbound. We were facing each other and she was shaking her fist at me. She had a vicious look on her face. I could see her mouth moving but I couldn't hear her. We were one car length away from each other. I yelled at the top of my voice, saying to her, 'You don't see what I see." I shook my fist at her with a frightened look on my face. She didn't see the man pointing a gun at me! She moved to the lane to her right to let me go on my way! Thank God, we didn't have a wreck.

When the congested traffic cleared, I returned to the southbound lanes. I sped away cautiously without going over the speed limit. It was 40 mph. I couldn't wait to get home fast enough. I stopped at a grocery store before going home. I shopped at the Food for Less market on Central Avenue and Rosecrans Avenue. It wasn't far from my house.

After I stopped at the market I parked, then turned off the ignition switch. I stay in the car, I was in a daze.

Before I closed my eyes, I looked at the clock on the dashboard it was 2:30 p.m. I was so exhausted. I thought I had only closed my eyes for a second. But when I opened my eyes again, I realized I had slept for an hour and a half. It was four o'clock. After I gained my strength, I proceeded to shop for a few items in the market. I went to the cashier, after she totaled my items on the cash register she said, "Ms. Are you okay?"

I said, yes, I'm okay now. The lady said, it looks like you just saw a ghost. Your eyes are all bugged, and your skin is looking gray. At that time, I began explaining about the guy who had a gun who was shooting at traffic. She said, thank God you made it out of there.

Thank you, Jesus, I know my guardian angel was with me, even after I disobeyed the voice of the LORD. I learned a valuable lesson that day: always obey the voice of the Lord. The LORD specifically pre-warned me to stay on the freeway to go home. I had no business going to the wig boutique, after God warned me to stay on the freeway.

Chapter 30b - Guided By Angel On 91 Freeway

When I was five years old, my mother taught me to memorize Bible scriptures. She said, it's very important to keep the word of God in our hearts. After I became an adult, I memorize quite a few scriptures so I could quote them while driving my car. In the Los Angeles area, we have a lot more cars than some other cities. One afternoon, I was driving from the Whole Foods Market on Crenshaw and Pacific Coast Highway headed home, and I was listening to my favorite gospel music on the radio. I was driving on Artesia Boulevard headed Eastward. I was just about to get on the 91 Freeway, when I heard the Holy Spirit speak to me. He said, "Give me some time." I knew what God meant. He needed me to turn off my music and give him some praise.

I turned the radio off right away, before getting onto the 91 Freeway. I pressed down on the gas pedal until I reached the speed of the traffic.

I remember, I had reached 65 miles per hour. I noticed a diesel truck driving on the right side of my car. I was catching up to a huge truck on the right side of my car, it was about 3 cars ahead of me. Suddenly, a large tarp flew off the truck. It flew up in the air and landed on my windshield.

It sounded like heard metal hit my windshield. But the amazing thing is that, I didn't have any fear.

When I obeyed God by turning off my music, then, I quoted Proverbs 3:5, and 6, "Trust in the Lord with all your heart, and lean not to your own understanding. In all your ways, acknowledge him, and he shall direct your path." It seemed like it was 5 minutes that my windshield was covered, but, I could've been only 10 seconds. I don't know. The point is, that when I started praising God, he took control of the steering wheel to keep me safe. When the tarp finally flew off my car. I safely drove to the shoulder of the Freeway to stop. I looked at my windshield, but it was not damaged at all.

Praise God for sending his angels to protect me. From that, I've learned to always put God first.

Chapter 30c - A Near Death Experience

I remember, the day when I felt death taking hold of me, I was frightened! I woke up on a Tuesday morning, I read my Bible as I do every day. I thanked God, and praised the Lord for a new day. It was March 26, 2002 at 8:00, I had my favorite breakfast ready for me to eat. It was a golden-brown sausage. I could taste the sage in it. I had two slices of crunchy toast that was golden brown with butter. I also had slices of sweet cantaloupe. I took one bite of my favorite food. After chewing it, I couldn't swallow.

I panicked! I took a napkin and wiped the food out of my mouth. I noticed that there was a clear white thick substance that came out of my mouth. It had the texture of Jell-O. I was feeling weak, I remembered, I put my hand over my heart. I could barely feel my heart beating. I felt my life was slipping away from me. I laid my head down on the table. I didn't have the strength to hold it up. I began to cry out in a pathetic weak voice, I cried God help me."

I had to whisper; my voice was getting weaker. I laid my head on the dining room table. I said, "Help me Jesus!" I had no idea of how ill I really was, all I know is that I never experienced feeling that weak ever until that day.

One of my younger sisters was living with me at that time. She was sitting nearby on the sofa watching television. The living room and the dining area are in the same room. My sister could see me and hear my faint voice.

I was so weak I couldn't hold my head up. With excitement in my sister's voice she said, "Kamiah are you, alright?" I could barely whisper. Instead of trying to force a sound out me I just shook my head no.

I cried out, "Jesus, Jesus, help me." My sister asked me again, "Are you doing all right?" I responded with a moaning sound, and next I begin to speak very slow as I slurred my words saying, "No, I-don't-feel-well. I took a deep breath! I cried out again and said, "Jesus help me!"

Suddenly, I felt a surge of energy come into my body. I felt air come into my lungs. I said to my sister, "I need to go to the doctor." In a split second, I saw a mental picture of a business card I had in my wallet. It was the card I received from a cashier at a Health Food Store. He gave it to me three months prior to this day. I called the telephone number to the Herbal Doctor's office that was on the card. The cashier had referred me to this doctor.

I went to the bedroom to get my wallet. I called the doctor's office! The receptionist answered the phone, then she transferred my call to the doctor! She said, "American Herbal and Medical Clinic. May I help you?" In a weak voice, I said, "I've been coughing up a clear thick fluid that has the texture of Jell-O, and I feel ill. The doctor asked, "How long have you had those symptoms?" I said, it just happened this morning. I tried to eat my breakfast. But I couldn't swallow my food. The doctor said, "The symptoms you are having are life threatening. I need you to get here immediately."

She asked, "How soon can you get here?" I answered, "I will be there right away." My heart began to beat with excitement; this time I could feel my heart beating stronger. I was afraid. I didn't know what to do. I asked God to help me.

I asked my sister to drive me to the doctor's clinic. She said that she couldn't because her driver's license had expired. I said a quick prayer. Jesus, I need you, please help me. After I prayed, I felt energetic! Then, I could dress myself.

Thank God, I could drive on the freeway, and it seemed like the LORD had cleared the highway for me. It wasn't a lot of cars out during the morning hours. Therefore, it took me about 20 minutes to get there. Thank God, we arrived at the clinic safe. The doctor's office was on the third floor.

As soon as I walked into the doctor's office, the Receptionist greeted me and handed me the admittance form to fill out.

The doctor admitted me into the hospital right away. I had to remove all my clothing for the examination. She rubbed my complete body with a warm ointment and wrapped me tightly into a warm sheet. Next, she gave me a cup of green liquid to drink. Before she left the room, she dimmed the lights. She told me to relax and rest. She'd check on me periodically. I fell asleep, and I could hear her gently calling my name. When I opened my eyes, the doctor had me sit up. She gave me more herbal tea to drink. That was a part of my treatment.

After the doctor had me drink three different herbal teas, she sent me to get my lab test done. The nurse transported me in a van. I lied down on a mattress because I was too weak to sit.

It didn't take long for my test because the doctor requested a rush. When I wanted peace of mind, I read: Isaiah 26:3. It says, "Thou wilt keep him in perfect peace whose mind is stayed on thee: because he trusts in thee." That scripture blessed me to have a piece of mind. I put all my trust in God because I knew worrying about my situation wouldn't be good for me.

The first day I stayed in the clinic, the doctor gave me liquids for my treatment. She was an herbal and medical doctor. I stayed in a cozy room; it had Scriptures typed on picture canvas backgrounds in beautiful frames hanging on the wall. There were stuffed teddy bears sitting on the twin size beds. My sister stayed there with me. She slept in a recliner. The next morning Dr. Koppertino awakened me so she could feed me solid foods.

She explained that she had 13 different types of foods for me to eat. She fed me one food at a time, just in case I had an allergic reaction. She informed me that there would be a possibility I may vomit and be very sick.

The doctor kept a record of the food and the time I ate. To her surprise, I had finished the test without getting sick. The doctor yelled out to the nurse and said, "She did not get sick." She did not know it, but I prayed to God saying, "Lord helps me not to get sick." Next the doctor gave me a strict menu diet for my blood type which she said would be the best foods for me to eat to help me recover from the illness.

I had been so ill it really didn't take me long to change my eating habits. It means life or death for me by the way I must eat. I had to change all my eating habits, compared to the way I used to eat. The doctor told the nurse that I had cancer, but I just ignored what the doctor said. I kept saying out loud, "I am healed by Jesus' stripes, I am healed, thank you Lord for healing me." The doctor thought I didn't hear what she said, so she said it again that I had cancer.

The doctor didn't know why I couldn't accept her report that I had cancer. But I read in the Bible that Jesus took illness for me, when he died on the cross. I believe God's word is true. It was by my faith that I was healed. That's why I didn't accept her report.

She said it again. She said it louder this time, as she told the nurse to record it on my chart. The doctor said, "Ms. Maury, you have cancer." I yelled! saying to the doctor, I am healed by Jesus' stripes. After I said I was healed by Jesus' stripes the second time, the doctor knew I wouldn't change my mind that I was healed. She told the nurse that I was crazy. She wrote me a prescription to take daily; then handed it to me. She tilted her head and rolled her eyes at me with an attitude. Then she gave me a list of foods that are for me to eat for my blood type.

I stayed in the hospital for four days and three nights. My sister stayed the entire time I was there. She was afraid to stay at my house alone. The doctor let her sleep on a lounge chair in my room. The doctor was getting ready to discharge me from the hospital. So she asked "Do you have someone to take care of you when you get home?"

I answered. Yes, my sister will help me. She needed a place to stay; so, I thought she would be there for me. But after I was home a week, she decided to go live with her son. My children were counting on her to be there to help me. They were furious when they found out she was leaving me. Fear rose in me big time!

I wondered, what am I going to do. My four children had jobs so they couldn't be there to take care of me. I started to pray, I knew God would help me make it through my illness.

I received a call from the receptionist at the doctor's office. She said, "The doctor says you only have 3 months to live." Was I afraid? Of course, I was. However, I thought that God didn't bring me this far to leave me. He said in his word that he'd never leave us nor forsake us.

When I stopped looking at my illness, I began to praise God instead. That was when I felt my body getting stronger. God had healed me. I didn't let the enemy to deviate my belief in God's Word. That happened to me in 2002. But praise God; Jesus healed me. I am still living in the year 2017 to tell my story.

Before I became ill, I was going to a well-known hospital. I will not mention the doctor's name. But the medication he prescribed was too strong for me. The name of medication is Calan. It was 180 mgs.

I had been a member of Pastors Walter and Margie's church, on October 1, 2002. I was there for five months then I became seriously ill. It was March 26, 2002, the doctor said I had cancer. But I refused to accept the doctor's report. I knew Jesus said he took all illnesses for us. I said out loud to the doctor, "I'm healed by Jesus 'stripes." I didn't want to accept the doctor's diagnosis about having cancer. So I got a second opinion. The second doctor said that I had a weak immune system.

I was happy to be well enough to return to church. I am excited to give my testimony that God healed me!

I took high blood pressure medication for fifteen years, but it wasn't helping me. It made me worse instead. I prayed and asked God to show the doctors why the medication was making me sick. God answered my prayer'. After I had the lab test, the doctor told me the results. He said, I was sensitive to the high blood pressure medications. Thank God! I haven't been in the emergency room since then.

My heart was beating so slow from the high blood pressure medication, the doctor sent me to the heart ward. First, he had the nurse to give me an injection in my stomach. It was a horrible experience being on the heart ward. It was noisy. There were bells ringing all night and all day. The lights were flashing night and day too. The nurses were laughing and talking about what they were going to do for the weekend. They were saying, what they were going to do when they got off work.

When the doctor examined my heart again it was beating normal. I believe while I was on the heart ward, all the noise that I heard must have helped my heart to start beating to the rhythm of life again. The doctor said that all my heart tests came back negative. I went back to my primary doctor, I told her that the medications were making me ill. She advised me to just stop taking them. I thank God that when I stopped taking the medications, I felt so much better.

I thank God, I found a doctor who advised me to eliminate salt from my diet. He advised exercise and to eat my own cooking, and to stop eating at restaurants. Then, I could stop taking high blood pressure medications. He advised me not to eat any body's cooking nor eat at restaurants. It was such a good feeling for me to get off high blood pressure medications. Plus, I didn't have to call the paramedics any more.

All the high blood pressure medications that I took, I had side effects from them. It caused me to go to the emergency room every three months.

I thank God that I've been off high blood pressure medication for twelve years now. God blessed me to find a doctor that finally listened to me. He said, "The only prescription I am going to prescribe for you is: I need you to cook your own food, stop eating out, and do not eat other people's cooking.

The doctor said, I need you to exercise every day and monitor your blood pressure every day. Is that clear?" I agreed to follow his instructions. I thank God that my blood pressure is doing well. I learned how to exercise while I do my housework. Thanks to the good LORD, I've keeping my weight down too. I give God all the glory, because He is the one who gives me the strength to do these things.

I take nutritious snacks with me where ever I go.

I've learned to look for the good in unhappy situations. I found the good in life even after going through my divorce. I learned that I can never lose someone I never had in the first place. Although I desired to stay married, he wanted the divorce. I've learned to enjoy family and friends more. I learned to make time for them, instead of never finding the time.

With the help of God, I expect to find happiness every day. I say, "This is the day which the LORD hath made; we will rejoice and be glad in it." Above all, I give God the glory and praise for sparing my life.

My sister moved out of my house when I needed her most. She promised my doctor that she would be there to take care of me so I could stay off my feet. I lost massive amounts of calcium from my body when I went through my illness.

At the time my sister left me, I didn't realize it then; but after she was gone it didn't take me too long to understand it was for my good. By being active it helped me to gain my strength back. I didn't have anyone to cook and clean my house for me. I was very weak. I had to drag a chair from my dining room to the kitchen and put a pillow in the chair so I could rest. I would stand up a few minutes at a time to prepare my food and then sit down and lay my head on the pillow.

The doctor advised me to eat only fresh vegetables. One day, I was washing some turnip greens in the kitchen sink and it clogged up. I had to dip the water out of the sink into a big pot, and carry it to the bathroom to empty it.

Every time I would uplift a pot of water, it was building up my strength. Then one day it was obvious that God orchestrated the time for my sister to leave me. Then I had to get out of bed to gain strength. When I thought I needed her most it really wasn't as bad as I thought it would be. It was great because I was gaining my strength back.

My testimony reminds me of the Bible scripture: Romans 8:28, "And we know that all things work together for good to them that love God, to them who are the called according to his purpose."

All I can say is that God knows what we need. Now, I can understand why I had to struggle back and forth to the kitchen. It was only to make me strong. As I sang praises to God five months had passed before I knew it. Finally, I realized that when I'd sing praises to God the time was going by faster. I enjoyed feeling the presence of the LORD. I read a scripture that says, the LORD inhabits the praises of His people. I can look back on those months and years as though it was a dream now. Even though I know it was real and it really did happen to me!

Chapter 30d Testimony - The Withered Rose Came Alive

My friend Mary is my sister in Christ Jesus. She is a caring person. She has prayed anointed prayers for me when I was ill. She has a spiritual ear to hear from the LORD. We met in 1997 at her relative's church. We became close friends since then. We'd visit patients in a convalescent home; we'd sing and read the Bible to them for over five years. When I became ill on March 26, 2002, she was always there to help me. She's a true friend.

Sister Mary was with me through my up and down days. It was three years later after I got better, she told me how my body looked to her when I first became ill. With a smile on her face she said, "Sister Kamiah when you first became ill, you resembled a withered rose. You had lost so much weight. Now that you have gained your weight back, praise God; you look like the rose that came back to life! We both begin to give thanks to God and praise Him for healing me. I said "Sister Mary, the way you described my appearance when I was ill was so beautiful! Thank you!"

Chapter 30e - Anointed By Great Nephew

I hope these testimonies will help strengthen your faith. One day in April 2002, while I was on my bed of affliction, I was frail and weak. My younger sister Darlene came to visit me. She brought her grandson Austin with her.

She said, "My grandson is anointed with the Holy Spirit. He came to anoint you with olive oil." He had faith I'd get well. He was nine years old at the time. I said to her that my doctor told me not to put anything on my body because my immune system was weak. She said that I shouldn't put anything on my skin but Ivory soap. Whatever I put on my skin could penetrate through my pores and get into my system. My sister said, "The olive oil won't hurt you. So let Austin anoint you so you can get well."

"No, I said. The doctor told me not to put anything on my body. That means no olive oil." My sister said a prayer over me and handed me a book of healing scriptures. After I had read a few paragraphs from the little book, I laid it beside me on the bed.

My great nephew Austin caught me off guard when I closed my eyes. He leaped upon the bed and landed his body across my chest. He dipped his fingers in olive oil and swiped it across my forehead in a split second. It happened so fast I didn't have time to say a word. To my surprise, after he had anointed me with the oil, I felt a surge of energy come into my body. My sister started shouting, "Hallelujah! Praise God, Thank you Jesus." She said, "I saw your flesh spring up from a look of death to a fountain of life after Austin anointed you." We began singing praises to God.

Later she said, "Girl, when we first saw you, you looked like flesh and bones. You lost so much weight. You resembled the cartoon Gumby, when he'd flatten his self out and slide under the crack of a door. (LOL) Of course, I had to laugh because of the way she described me.

Even in a serious situation, my sister has the personality to make a person laugh when it's nothing funny. I had a mental picture of how Gumby the cartoon character looked. It made me laugh so hard. I believe the laughter made me feel better. I learned that God can heal through a child's faith on behalf of another person. I thank God for my great nephew Austin. I thank God that my sister brought him with her to heal me by using his faith in God. Thank you, Jesus.

Chapter 30f - Great-Grand Daughter's Prayer

On Thanksgiving Day, I had my children, grandchildren, and great grandchildren over for dinner. Everyone was enjoying their dinner. Except for me. My great granddaughter Qiana was very mature for her age. With a concerned look on her face, she looked at me. She asked, "Great grandma, how come you're not eating your dinner?"

I was so sick; I could only eat raw foods. I couldn't digest meat. I had side effects from the medication a doctor prescribed me. After I took it for several years, I became very ill. In 1999, I first noticed that my health was declining. Before I took medication, I ate all kinds of food. I didn't have any allergies either.

I answered my great granddaughter and said, "Honey, I can't eat cooked food because it makes me sick." She stopped eating; she laid her fork on the table. She held her hands together in a praying position. She started to pray. She said, "Dear Jesus, please help great-grandma to eat food like us, Amen! We all looked at each other in amazement. Qiana was 5 at the time. She was the youngest one at the dinner table. But she knew how to pray a sincere prayer.

I didn't get to eat right away; it was two weeks that had past that I realized God had healed my digestive system. Then I could eat meat again. I called My'esa who is my granddaughter and Qiana's mother to tell her that I can eat meat again. With excitement in my voice I said, "My'esa, let me speak to Qiana." Little Qiana listened on the telephone while I said "Qiana, your great grandma can eat now."

She was excited too. She said "Mommy! Great grandma can eat now." We praised the LORD the rest of the day. God will answer the prayers of anyone who has a sincere heart.

Chapter 30g - Prayer Answered By Deacon And Wife

When my husband divorced me, I had no sufficient income. But God provided for me!. (Philippians 4:19, says, "But my God shall supply all your need according to his riches in glory by Christ Jesus."

My income was only $399.00 a month, from S.S.I. I had no other income. I needed dental work done, but I couldn't afford the gold crown that cost $200.00. The dentist said, I had to have the gold crown for my tooth in the back of my mouth. I said a prayer; I asked God to make a way for me to pay for it. I said, "Heavenly Father, you said in your word that you would supply all my needs according to your riches in glory by Christ Jesus. I never uttered a word to anyone about my situation except to the LORD!

It was two weeks after I had prayed, a Deacon in my church said to me, "Minister Maury, God told me to give you this." He had his hand closed. I responded, well if God spoke to you about giving me something, then I must accept it.

He reached his closed hand toward my hand to put some money in it. I was shocked to see in my hand a $100.00 bill. I shook his hand and thanked him. He walked away. But in a short while he returned with his wife. He said, Minister Maury, I'm sorry I didn't give you all that God told me to give you. He reached out his closed hand again to me. He said, "Here's the rest of the money I am supposed to give you."

I opened my hand to receive the money. He said he was nervous; but this is the rest of the money God told me to give you. It was another $100.00 bill that he gave me. It was exactly what I needed. I thanked the Deacon and his wife for obeying God. When I got home, I wept with tears of joy. God has shown me that He is with me and has never left me. He's been with me all my life, even when I wasn't aware of it. Hallelujah, thank you LORD! However, as I wrote my story God revealed to me that He has been with me all my life.

Chapter 30h - Extraordinary Neighbor

In 2006, one morning I sat up in the bed to read my Bible as I usually do every day. I turned to the side of the bed and placed my feet on the floor to put on my slippers. When I stood up and took a few steps, I noticed that my legs were shaky and weak. My equilibrium was off. I grabbed hold of the wall. Fear came over me! I didn't know what was wrong with me. I called on my neighbor Sellie; she drove me to the hospital. Wait a minute! She went the extra mile. She spent the night with me in the hospital. She slept on the end of my bed. Whenever I needed to go to the restroom, she'd help me walk there. She was heaven sent. She did something you'd think a relative would do! Thank you Sister Sellie for being there for me! May God bless you always. I had to share this testimony because I never had a neighbor sacrifice their time to be by my side like she did.

Chapter 30i - Now I Get To Know Him

I cried tears because of a broken heart, when my husband divorced me. I knelt on my knees by the bedside. While crying, I took the time to pray. I cried, LORD! Our Heavenly Father, this divorce hurts me so badly. While still crying, I read a scripture out loud to God. I cried! LORD, according to Romans 8:28, "And we know that all things work together for good to them that love God, to them who are the called according to his purpose."

With tears streaming down my face, I asked God a question; "LORD please show me the good that is coming out of my divorce?" He answered me in an audible voice saying, "NOW YOU GET TO KNOW ME! The sound of his voice was above my head; just like it was coming from the ceiling! It was the most amazing experience to hear his distinct and melodic voice.

I felt His love surround me as the pain left my heart. There was no doubt in my mind that I heard God's voice. Wow! I was excited to get to know Him. Psalm 34:18 says, "The LORD is nigh unto them that are of a broken heart; and saves such as be of a contrite spirit."

After, God said, "NOW YOU GET TO KNOW ME," I stopped crying tears of sadness; then I cried tears of joy. I realized, I had put my husband above Him. S, this time I asked him to forgive me. I quoted the scripture back to him that says, "But seek ye first the kingdom of God, and his righteousness and all these things shall be added unto you." God wants us to depend upon Him!

Chapter 30j - Facing Health Issues

While I was teaching at three schools, I enrolled in a computer class part time to enhance my job skills. One of those schools was a community college where I taught the Kollege for Kids program. I taught several hundred children during the summer sessions. I thank God for blessing me with the best job I ever had.

I had medical insurance with a major hospital; they increased my medical insurance so high that I couldn't afford it. But when I cancelled my medical insurance, it was the best decision I made.

The reason is because when I was a patient at a medical clinic, I had an Oriental doctor that was very mean to me. I had a pain in the middle of my chest; I told him about it. While he was examining me, he took his two fingers and rammed them as hard as he could into my chest. He said, "Is this where it hurts?" That doctor didn't show any compassion at all.

I went to a herbal doctor, I had to pay cash for my visits. This was a challenge for me not knowing what was wrong. I had to put my trust in God to make a way for me to pay the doctor because I didn't have medical insurance.

Therefore, I used my credit card to purchase the herbs. I called on the doctor of all doctors. I called on Doctor Jesus, who is the healer and the greatest physician of all.

After the side effects from medications made me sick, I went to see a herbal doctor. The doctor prescribed herbal medicines for me to cleanse my body from the side effects from the medication. I was taking a medication called Calan. It was 180 mg. I started to feel better after I took the herbs.

He advised me to eat 80% of raw foods and 20% cooked foods which I did. Then I became medication free. I still had the pain in the center of my chest. I asked, why am I still having chest pains? He said, "Young lady, it takes time for our bodies to heal so you need to be patient while your body heals."

I continued to eat raw foods and less cooked foods, and one day the pain was gone. The cooked foods that I ate were oatmeal with raisins, boiled eggs and toast, and I'd have a baked potato with a vegetarian sausage occasionally. That was the diet that I ate for a year. I didn't realize that I had serious problems going on in my body. After eating the way, the herbal doctor had advised me to eat; I was still feeling ill. But I realized that it takes time. So I had to dwell on being patient.

I gave him a call and told him, I wasn't feeling well. He told me that there was nothing more he could do for me. He said, sometimes we all must learn how to be our own doctor. After the herbal doctor told me that there was nothing else he could do I was frightened! I started crying. Then I called on the LORD to show me what to eat. Because of that I started getting ideas about purchasing books on medical health and health food books. I've learned that we cannot depend totally on the doctors for our health.

I realized first to seek God's wisdom and advice. How do we do that? I'm glad you asked. (Smiles,) Well since God created everything, the Bible tells us in Matthew 7:7, "Ask, and it shall be given you; seek and ye shall find; knock, and it shall be opened unto you." I am learning that God is waiting for us to ask Him for the things in life that will please Him, and things that are good for us too.

In the summer of 2001, I was working at Compton Community College. One of the parents and I became friends. She said, "Ms. Maury, you are losing too much weight! Please don't lose any more!" "Oh, I'm doing alright!" She said Okay, take care of yourself. I really didn't realize that I had lost so much weight because I felt great. It's good to have people in our lives that don't mind speaking the truth to us!

Chapter 30k - God's Never Late

We know that God is never late, He's always on time. My son thought I gave him away when he was a baby, but I didn't. God brought my son Michael back into my life about three years ago. He is now 59 years old and every time he calls me he says, "I love you Mom." He used to be angry with me. God is so amazing how He mends the wounded hearts and brings families back together.

Chapter 30l - Never Give Up

I thank God for healing me. I survived three near death experiences. I learned valuable lessons from two divorces. I didn't let it ruin the rest of my life. After being divorced for 22 years, I learned that there is life after a divorce.

Never give up on life, live life one day at a time! We must choose to enjoy life every moment. It doesn't just happen by itself. Look for the good in every experience you have. That's when I began to enjoy life; by letting go of things I cannot change.

Summary

"ANGELS PROTECTED ME"

An amazing thing happened to me, As I started writing my story on February 12, 2010. I was going through trials; but I didn't understand why I had so many of them.

I learned that they teach us about life. If we never had a problem, we'd never have a reason to call on God. He's the creator of the universe; he wants us to get to know him. He is the one who helps us solve our problems.

I was age 69 when I began writing my story. I found out God sent my angels to protect me. When the girls from the reform school tried to rape me, they didn't succeed because my angels protected me.

In 2002, the doctor said I had three months to live. That was her report; but I didn't receive it. I know that Jesus took sin and sickness for us. That's why I say, by faith I'm healed. By God's grace, I am still here in 2017. Praise God!

As you read this story, I hope it will strengthen your faith to know that there is nothing impossible with GOD.

When we call on him; God sends his angels to protect us from harm!

How would we know God could solve our problems if we never had one. Through problems was when I found out the greatness of God.

When we look for the good in our problems, we can find it. If we look for the bad, we can find that too.

Conclusion

This memoir is about giving God all the glory of what he has brought me through. The purpose for this book is to encourage others. God wants us to depend on him because he has all the answers to our problems. It's great to know that we have a choice in our journey. My favorite Scripture: Psalm 11:24, This is the day the LORD has made; we will rejoice and be glad in it!" Now that I know my angels protect me, I will choose to rejoice every day, in the Lord.

Every day I thank God that Jesus healed me. I thank God's angels protected me from those that tried to do me harm. Praise God!

I promised my children that I'd tell my story the way it happened, but I'm in no way proud of my past life. My oldest son Michael said, "Mom, don't feel bad about what happened in your past; that's your history." I said, I was just a teenager; I made a lot of mistakes that I'm not proud of! I responded. Well, I WASN'T PERFECT. "Mom, I love you because you are my Mommy! I want to know your history!"

The tragedies I've gone through gave me the chance to test my faith. How do you know how strong your faith is unless you've had it tested? It helped me to know that God is real. It was my worst and best experience at the same time. The worst part of having problems is not knowing how to handle them. When we find out how awesome our creator is, that's the best part of a problem. He shows up and shows out to fix our problems for us. Only when we ask for his help.

God sent his angels to protect me in every situation. Each time I faced death, he spared me. When people did me wrong, I prayed, and God fought my battles for me. My purpose in life is to share with others that God and angels are real. That's why I share my story with all that want to hear it. I'm blessed to still be here. I'm blessed to still have a sound mind, after all I've been through. Thank God! Everybody has a story. When are you going to tell yours?

THE END